DISPENSATIONALISM

AND

FREE GRACE

Intimately 🔗 Linked

GRANT HAWLEY

Scripture taken from the New King James Version®.
Copyright © 1982 by Thomas Nelson. Used by permission. All rights reserved.

Printed in the United States of America

First Edition, First Printing, 2017

ISBN: 978-1-945774-14-0

Dispensational Publishing House, Inc.
PO Box 3181
Taos, NM 87571

www.dispensationalpublishing.com

Ordering Information:
Quantity sales. Special discounts are available on quantity purchases by churches, associations, and others. For details, contact the publisher at the address above.

Orders by U.S. trade bookstores and wholesalers. Please contact the publisher:
Tel: (844) 321-4202

1 2 3 4 5 6 7 8 9 10

This book is dedicated with love and thanks to my parents, whose love for me has always been unconditional. Their example helps me to understand our Heavenly Father's love, and I am blessed to be their son.

ENDORSEMENTS

When people ask me how I became free grace in my views, I tell them that there was no conversion. I just read the Bible and let it speak for itself. For the same reason, I was a dispensationalist before I knew what the word was. Grant Hawley really nails down this connection between taking the Bible literally in context, dispensationalism, and free grace. He does it carefully and argues forcefully. I appreciate the historical perspective this book brings and hope that it is read widely so that people can better understand how modern controversies evolved. This short book is a full education about the foundation of free grace theology. It is essential reading.

Charles C. Bing – Director, GraceLife Ministries

Free grace and dispensationalism are intimately linked by their coherence and consistency in the Scriptures. In an age where scholars have largely bypassed careful exegesis and interpretation in favor of applications derived from a spiritualized and cultural hermeneutic, few works are seeking to turn the tides of such irresponsibility in handling the Word of God. Thankfully, this book stands in the gap. Hawley's work on this subject is well-researched, accessible and timely; an open and closed case if there ever was one.

Jeremy Edmondson – Pastor, Grace Bible Church, Portage, Wis.

More than a decade ago we wrote that free grace is a corollary of consistent dispensationalism. Why? Because only dispensationalism separates the judgment seat of Christ for believers from the great white throne for unbelievers. But we didn't devote much ink to support the claim. Grant Hawley does exactly that by demonstrating the convergent histories of free grace and dispensationalism. Where dispensationalism goes, free grace is sure to follow, assuming a consistent hermeneutic. Hawley does a great job of explaining why this is true.

David R. Anderson – President, Grace School of Theology

The change in Augustine's soteriology based on his change to amillennialism led Grant Hawley on an intriguing investigation of present-day scholars. As a result, he shows a natural correspondence between covenant theology and Lordship salvation. This survey of authors is worth your consideration concluding that normative dispensationalism and free grace also naturally correspond.

Elliott Johnson – Senior professor of Bible exposition, Dallas Theological Seminary

Grant Hawley has provided a much needed explanation of the historical and theological backgrounds of free grace theology. He clearly demonstrates how the dispensational commitment to a literal hermeneutic leads naturally to a free grace view of soteriology. On the other hand, he explains how a non-literal hermeneutic results in Lordship soteriology. If the central purpose of Biblical history is the salvation of man, as covenant theology maintains, they have great difficulties explaining the many passages of Scripture which describe a judgment on believers according to works. Their non-literal hermeneutic leads naturally to an abandonment of a future earthly kingdom. Therefore, the judgment of the believer's works at the judgment seat of Christ becomes a judgment instead on unbelievers and is merged with the judgment on unbelievers at the great white throne judgment. Thus, works become either a condition of salvation or a test of its genuineness. With relentless logic and Biblical discussion, Grant connects free grace theology with one's millennial views; the setting aside of the Mosaic law for believers today; and how believers can find assurance. He points out how God's faithfulness to His promises to Israel, even though they became unfaithful, naturally leads to His faithfulness to us, even when we also fail. I have learned much from reading this interesting and helpful volume. You will too!

Joseph Dillow – Author, *Final Destiny: The Future Reign of the Servant Kings*

Table of Contents

PROLOGUE

A Note from the Author

About a decade ago I was introduced to free grace theology. At that time I understood *discipleship* to mean "being a Christian," *the kingdom* to often mean "the church," *reward* to mean "free gift," *free gift* to mean "conditional gift," *justified by works* (from James 2) to mean "justified by faith evidenced by works" and *believe* to mean whatever I wanted it to mean at the time.[1] When I was introduced to free grace, I started seeing scholars like Joseph Dillow, Zane Hodges and Bob Wilkin use the term *kingdom* to mean "kingdom," *believe* to mean "believe," *reward* to mean "reward," etc., and I was dumbfounded. My thought process went something like, "This may provide an answer to the contradictions I was growing uncomfortable with, but do we have to *redefine* everything to make it work?" The irony certainly does not escape me.

It was not long until I realized that the Bible was really a much simpler book than I had imagined, and that it really was written to be understood. A non-literal approach to Scripture is largely responsible for the widespread confusion and the resulting reluctance of the layperson to study the Bible without undue dependence upon commentaries. The popularity of paraphrases and dynamic equivalence versions of the Bible such as *The Message*[2] and the New International Version[3] is largely due to this misconception, and reflects a growing pre-Reformational attitude that the unlearned cannot be trusted with the Word of God without a mediator.[4]

I have found over the last several years that much of the task of a free grace teacher is simply to unravel the confusion woven by a long tradition of non-literal interpretation, to help students pay attention to context, and to let words mean what they say. In doing so, I am reminded of dispensational works such as *Prophecy Made Plain* by C. I. Scofield,[5] in which the author shows that prophecy is not impossible to understand if we simply pay attention to context and let the principle of literal interpretation rule. Soteriology is no different.

As a pastor, I have introduced many people to free grace theology in discipleship settings, and those who have accepted it have *without fail* commented that free grace makes the Bible much easier to understand. This has long been recognized as a benefit of dispensationalism as well. This is plainly admitted in Arthur Pink's introduction to his work against dispensationalism:

> [Dispensationalism is] a device wherein the wily serpent appears as an angel of light, feigning to "make the Bible a new book" *by simplifying much in it which perplexes the spiritually unlearned* (emphasis added).[6]

In Pink's understanding, the simplicity and accessibility afforded by dispensationalism is outweighed by the desire to apply every portion of Scripture directly to the church age. Thus, covenant theology's unification of Scripture was preferable to him. I have found this to be a common theme (at least to some extent) among many (perhaps all) who have written in defense of Lordship salvation. This is true even among Lordship salvation proponents who embrace some form of dispensationalism. This will be demonstrated in the present book.

In the first chapter, I will demonstrate that many of the proponents of Lordship salvation have advanced the argument that normative dispensationalism and free grace go hand-in-hand. Among these are Drs. John MacArthur[7] and John Gerstner, though many others have also made this claim. I agree with this assertion.

To establish this connection, I will show where MacArthur and Gerstner have drawn a correlation between dispensationalism and free grace in their works on soteriology, and I will do a brief survey of the writings of A. W. Pink both before and after his change from dispensationalism to covenant theology, showing that his soteriology was greatly impacted by the change. In other words, in the first chapter, I hope to show that Lordship salvation comes out of an approach to interpretation that differs from the approach of normative dispensationalism.

In the second chapter, I will attempt to show how this occurs by interacting with specific methods of interpretation used by proponents of Lordship salvation as they are applied to various Biblical passages.

In the last chapter, I will attempt to demonstrate how and why dispensationalism has led so many to free grace theology.

CHAPTER 1

Dispensationalism: The Root Cause of Free Grace

Background and Need for the Present Study

Dave Anderson's articles in the *Journal of the Grace Evangelical Society*, "The Soteriological Impact of Augustine's Change from premillennialism to amillennialism: Parts 1 and 2,"[8] demonstrated conclusively that Augustine's abandonment of premillennialism produced a profound change in his soteriology. Out of an amillennial interpretation of Matthew 24:13, "But he who endures to the end shall be saved," Augustine's doctrine of perseverance of the saints was born and perseverance in faithful obedience became a condition for final salvation. Naturally, the reformer John Calvin—who depended heavily upon Augustine for his doctrine— adopted both amillennialism and perseverance of the saints. Calvin's work has obviously had a profound impact on many.

Building upon Anderson's conclusions, I will attempt to show that premillennialism is only one of many aspects of dispensationalism that has a significant impact on soteriology, as can be shown by the near universal acceptance of Lordship salvation among covenant premillennialists. The cause-and-effect relationship between dispensationalism and free grace is so clear that dispensationalism is regularly attacked in works on soteriology written from the Lordship salvation perspective. I will demonstrate in this work that this is a legitimate connection because, unless many essential tenets of normative dispensationalism are abandoned, Lordship salvation cannot be maintained.

Before proceeding, a definition of normative dispensationalism is necessary. While normative dispensationalists disagree on various things, virtually all would agree upon the following points:

1. Literal, historical, grammatical interpretation should be applied to *all* portions of Scripture.

2. The church and Israel are distinct peoples in God's program for the ages.

3. The Lord Jesus Christ will return bodily to earth and reign on David's throne in Jerusalem for 1,000 years.

4. The underlying purpose of God's dealings with the world is His glory, not merely the salvation of man, and thus the Scripture goes far beyond evangelism.[9]

5. The Christian is free from the law[10] in its entirety for both justification (Gal 2:16) and sanctification (Gal 5:18).[11]

When discussing normative dispensationalism, these descriptions will define my usage. This is expanded from Ryrie's *sine qua nons*[12] in order to distinguish normative dispensationalism from other dispensational views.

A study of this nature is especially relevant today because dispensationalism is becoming more and more rare. Progressive dispensationalism (a system which departs from dispensationalism in key areas[13]) is replacing normative dispensationalism in some historically dispensational seminaries, including Dallas Theological Seminary, which produces hundreds of graduates who go on to become pastors every year.

And while there are some non-dispensational free grace scholars (R. T. Kendall would be one example), free grace is extremely uncommon among non-dispensationalists[14] because free grace is largely dependent upon the principles of literal interpretation and careful attention to historical context that are fundamental to dispensationalism.

In this work, I will provide a brief survey of the ways in which dispensationalism has come under attack in the soteriological literature produced by some key proponents of Lordship salvation,[15] followed by a look at how various non-dispensational approaches to interpretation have yielded Lordship salvation in these and other authors. Lastly, I will argue that Lordship salvation does not hold up under consistent dispensationalism and that free grace is the natural outcome of a consistently literal interpretation of Scripture.

Before proceeding, I want to be careful to note that I do not believe that every consistent dispensationalist is consistently free grace. Many consistent dispensationalists hold to a soft perseverance of the saints viewpoint, stating that every true believer will produce *some* good works. This is usually based on their understanding of James 2:14-26. My contention is that Lordship salvation, an extreme view, cannot hold up under dispensationalism and that dispensationalism *most naturally* results in consistent free grace.

This work is not intended to be an exhaustive defense of dispensationalism,[16] but is simply to show that free grace and consistent, normative dispensationalism are intimately linked. It is my hope that this work will encourage further study by more capable scholars.

John MacArthur and Dispensationalism

John MacArthur clearly identifies as a dispensationalist in both *The Gospel According to Jesus*[17] and *The Gospel According to the Apostles*.[18] There is no doubt that he does hold to the fundamental distinction between the church and Israel (though he does not always apply this division consistently), and in surveying his works, I have never found anything to suggest otherwise. I want to state clearly that I take MacArthur's statements here at face value and do believe MacArthur to be a dispensationalist of sorts. However, as will be shown, the view he presents in *The Gospel According to Jesus* and elsewhere is not consistent with, and is even hostile to, *normative* dispensationalism.

Dispensationalism has come under attack (and suffered much) as a result of the Lordship salvation controversy, as MacArthur recognizes:

> The lordship debate has had a devastating effect on dispensationalism. Because no-lordship theology [note: a pejorative term for free grace] is so closely associated with dispensationalism, many have imagined a cause-and-effect relationship between the two.[19]

One of the most obvious examples of attacks on dispensationalism based on soteriology is Gerstner's book, *Wrongly Dividing the Word of Truth*, especially chapters 11-13.[20] Another is Reginald Kimbro's anti-dispensational work *The Gospel According to Dispensationalism*,[21] which patterns its name after MacArthur's *The Gospel According to Jesus*. Anecdotally, when I was speaking with a friend about free grace, I had encouraged her to look into some of Lewis Sperry Chafer's works. The following week, she told me that when she asked for them at her church library, she was told all of Chafer's books had been banned in their church after the publishing of *The Gospel According to Jesus*.

It is difficult to see that the attacks on dispensationalism that followed *The Gospel According to Jesus* were merely an unintended consequence. The words *dispensationalism* and *dispensationalist* are a common occurrence in the book,[22] and there are only two short paragraphs[23] in which the words were used in a positive sense. Even in those cases, MacArthur is careful to associate only with one tenet of dispensationalism (the separation of the church and Israel),[24] and these brief paragraphs are sandwiched between an open critique of normative dispensationalism.

In fact, MacArthur repeatedly and directly condemns many of the fundamentals of normative dispensationalism. One quote in particular has gained some attention:

> There is a tendency, however, for dispensationalists to get carried away with compartmentalizing truth to the point that they can make unbiblical distinctions. An almost obsessive desire to categorize everything neatly has lead various dispensationalist interpreters to draw hard lines not only between the church and Israel, but also between *salvation and discipleship, the church and the kingdom, Christ's preaching and the apostolic message, faith and repentance, and the age of law and the age of grace* (emphasis added).[25]

This quote is particularly relevant because it appears in the first chapter, entitled, "A Look at the Issues," and is presented as foundational to his argument. Elsewhere, MacArthur criticizes the distinction between "the gospel of the kingdom" and "the gospel of the grace of God" found in the *Scofield Reference Bible*.[26] Throughout *The Gospel According to Jesus*, Luke 19:10 is used by MacArthur to suggest that all of Jesus' teachings were related to the offer of eternal life.[27] This reveals MacArthur's soteriological view of history, the view of covenant theology, as opposed to the doxological priority view of dispensationalism.

In his criticism of dispensationalism on pages 31 and 32,

MacArthur also insists that dispensationalists teach different means of justification salvation in the various dispensations (by law-keeping in the age of law and by grace through faith in the age of grace). While there were some statements made by Chafer and Scofield which left some with this impression, those statements were later revised or clarified so that their clear intentions were evident.[28] Every normative dispensationalist that I am aware of teaches that justification by grace through faith has been God's program since the fall of man.[29]

Lastly, MacArthur's criticism of specific writers is reserved exclusively for dispensational scholars such as Chafer, Ryrie, Hodges, Constable, Scofield, Wilkin, and Thieme, while quoting from nearly 40 non-dispensational (and often quite anti-dispensational) scholars, and only one dispensationalist[30] for support in his disparagement of free grace. Many times, the specific works criticized were written in defense of dispensationalism.[31] The reasons stated above, along with one major purpose of *The Gospel According to Jesus* being to proclaim a non-dispensational view of Jesus' earthly ministry, have led many, including the present author, to conclude that it is as much an attack on normative dispensationalism as it is an attack on free grace.[32]

In *The Gospel According to the Apostles*, MacArthur is careful to express that it is only "one arm of the dispensationalist movement"[33] that promotes the free grace message. Later, he openly states that it is the dispensationalism of Chafer that has yielded free grace theology:

Who are the defenders of no-lordship dispensationalism? Nearly all of them stand in a tradition that has its roots in the teaching of Lewis Sperry Chafer. I will show in Appendix 2 that Dr. Chafer is the father of modern no-lordship teaching. Every prominent figure on the no-lordship side descends from Dr. Chafer's spiritual lineage. Though Dr. Chafer did not invent or originate any of the key elements of no-lordship teaching, he codified the system of dispensationalism on which all contemporary no-lordship doctrine is founded. That system is the common link between those who attempt to defend no-lordship doctrine on theological grounds."[34]

This is precisely the point that I have been making.

In his appendix entitled "What is Dispensationalism," MacArthur is careful to define his dispensationalism as dealing with the separation of the church and Israel only. He states, *"Dispensationalism is a system of biblical interpretation that sees a distinction between God's program for Israel and His dealings with the church.* It's really as simple as that"[35] (italics in original). It is, then, only by excluding all other elements of dispensationalism that MacArthur accepts the label "dispensationalist."

More recently, MacArthur has claimed the term "leaky dispensationalist" and has often stated plainly that he is much closer to covenant theologians than he is to most dispensationalists. In an interview with John Piper and Justin Taylor, MacArthur states:

When I wrote [*The Gospel According to Jesus*] I didn't know anybody outside of my circles really, and I didn't know how this book would be received. But Jim Boice agreed to write the foreword, and John Piper wrote an endorsement that was absolutely stunning to me, because I was really not moving in Reformed circles at that time. I was a leaky dispensationalist. That was my world, and I realized that I was much more one of you than I was one of them.[36]

In other words, the more MacArthur is entrenched in Lordship salvation, the more he finds himself identifying with non-dispensationalists rather than dispensationalists. This can also be seen in his regular appearances at the Ligonier conference and with other non-dispensational groups.[37] It is strange, then, that MacArthur would state that the connection between the two was simply imagined.[38] If the cause-and-effect relationship between dispensationalism and free grace is imagined, why would he have been so adamant about rejecting many aspects of dispensationalism in his books about soteriology? Why would MacArthur find himself more closely allied with anti-dispensationalists? And why would MacArthur adopt terms like "leaky dispensationalist" to define his views? Surely the connection between dispensationalism and free grace is more than coincidental.

John Gerstner

In *Wrongly Dividing the Word of Truth*, Gerstner makes a compelling case that dispensationalism has led to free grace theology, which he has incorrectly labeled as *antinomianism*.[39] Taken as a discussion of the soteriological differences between covenant theology and dispensationalism, it is a valuable tool. In it, however, only one brief chapter is devoted to dispensational hermeneutics, and this chapter is adapted from his earlier work.[40] While recognizing that dispensationalists do tend more toward literal interpretation, Gerstner rejects the claim that dispensationalism is primarily the fruit of a literal approach to Scripture and asserts that the theology is primary for the dispensationalist, rather than hermeneutics.[41] Gerstner makes the same claim in *A Primer on Dispensationalism*, but in it he admits that this is an unsure conclusion:

> It is very difficult to say which is the cart and which is the horse in this case. Is it the literalistic tendency that produces this divided Scripture, or is it the belief in a divided Scripture that drives the dispensationalist to ultra-literalism at some point? I think it is the latter, though that is not easy to prove.[42]

In *Wrongly Dividing the Word of Truth*, Gerstner seems to be more confident, but his argument is based upon an incorrect definition of literal interpretation (that literal interpretation does not recognize figures of speech) and demonstrates where dispensationalists depart from it. This is nothing more than the burning of a straw man.

In actuality, Gerstner commits the error that he is accusing the dispensationalists of committing. In *Wrongly Dividing the Word of Truth*, Gerstner largely bases his critique of dispensationalism upon its departure from TULIP Calvinism and fails to address it exegetically.[43] The essential flaw is that the force of his argument starts with soteriology and critiques dispensationalism, which is distinguished primarily by its hermeneutics,[44] upon theological ground, rather than upon hermeneutical differences. Gerstner's methodology of starting with soteriology and working backward from there has come under criticism even among those who share his soteriology.[45] It is clear that his methodology in this work is fundamentally flawed as an argument against dispensationalism. For this reason, *Wrongly Dividing the Word of Truth* is more appropriately seen primarily as a theological argument against the soteriology that is born of dispensationalism.

In the next chapter, I will address Gerstner's argument that theology is primary for the dispensationalist[46] rather than literal hermeneutics. But for now, it will suffice to show that, for Gerstner, dispensationalism and free grace go hand-in-hand.

Arthur Pink

Arthur Pink, champion of Reformed theology, was a dispensationalist early in his writing career. Pink wrote four books on the subject of premillennialism from a dispensational-premillennialist perspective.[47] The most well-known of these books is *The Redeemer's Return*, where Pink stresses the importance of Christ's imminent return and a pretribulational rapture.[48]

It may surprise some to know, however, that when Arthur Pink was a dispensationalist, he also embraced free grace, as is demonstrated in the following statement:

> Are you constrained to ask, "What must I do to be saved?"
> Then the answer, *God's* own answer, is ready to hand —
> "*Believe* on the Lord Jesus Christ and thou shalt be saved."
> Appropriate the provision which Divine grace has made for
> lost sinners.[49]

This is only one of many of Pink's clear statements regarding the free nature of the gift of eternal life.

Pink was not the beneficiary of more recent free grace scholarship that has helped to clarify many issues and terms. This is apparent in his use of phrases such as "salvation of the soul" to mean "deliverance from the wrath to come," and in his description of the believer as one who has "received the Lord Jesus Christ as his or her personal Saviour."[50] What he means by these phrases, however, is expressly defined in the context and completely consistent with free grace. Simple faith in Christ was the only condition Pink ever presented as necessary for receiving eternal life during his works written as a dispensationalist.

Furthermore, Pink made several astute observations that demonstrate sophistication of understanding in soteriological issues from the free grace perspective. For example, Pink speaks of the "present-tense aspect of our salvation" and further describes the believer's secure position based upon John 5:24: "Eternal life is something which every believer in Christ already possesses, and for him there is no possibility of future condemnation in the sense of having to endure God's wrath."[51] He then goes on to describe the different aspects of salvation:

In the New Testament the word 'Salvation' [sic] has a three-fold scope—past, present and future, which, respectively, has reference to our deliverance from the penalty, the power, and the presence of sin.[52]

Pink understood salvation as a broad concept that involves much more than justification before God.

Pink did not write a great deal of material about the judgment seat of Christ. He did, however, state its importance and describe the nature of it being to test the works of believers to determine reward. He states: "... the *purpose* of the appearing of believers 'before the Bema of Christ' is not to test their title and fitness for Heaven, but in order that their works may be examined and their service rewarded."[53] In this discussion, he expounds on 2 Corinthians 5:10 and 1 Corinthians 3:11-15, showing that they are not related to eternal destiny but to reward. He also references Matthew 25:23; 1 Corinthians 9:25; 2 Timothy 4:8; Hebrews 6:10; 1 Peter 5:4; and Revelation 2:10; 22:12, and alludes to the parable of the talents as related to the *Bema*.[54]

Finally, Pink also demonstrated that, for him, grace should be properly understood in light of the special nature of the present dispensation:

> Let us settle it once for all that the Dispensation in which we are living is a unique one, that it is fundamentally different from all that have preceded it and from that which is to follow it—the Millennium. This is the Dispensation of Grace, and grace obliterates all distinctions, grace eliminates all

questions of merits; grace makes every blessing a Divine and free gift. . . . Again we say, let us settle it once for all that we are living in the Dispensation of Grace (John 1:17; Eph. 3: 2) and that every blessing we enjoy is a gift of Divine clemency. We are justified by grace (Rom. 3:24). We are saved by grace (Eph. 2:8). The Holy Scriptures are termed "The Word of His Grace" (Acts 20:32). The Third Person of the Holy Trinity is denominated "The Spirit of Grace" (Heb. 10:29). God is seated upon a Throne of Grace (Heb. 4:16). And, the Good Hope which is given us is "through grace" (2 Thess. 2:16). It is all of Grace from first to last. It is all of Grace from beginning to end. It was grace that predestinated us before the world began (2 Tim. 1:9), and it will be grace that makes us like Christ at the consummation of our salvation. Thank God for such a "Blessed Hope."[55]

To this, every dispensational, free grace believer can give an enthusiastic, "Amen!" Dispensationalism clearly lead Pink to embrace grace "from first to last."

When Pink abandoned dispensationalism, however, he also abandoned free grace. The one-time proponent of the simplicity of justification by faith alone now asserts, "Something more than 'believing' is necessary to salvation."[56] Though he had once used John 5:24 and Acts 16:31 as the basis for the believer's assurance, he now refers to the one basing his assurance upon these verses as "Mr. Carnal Confidence"[57] and asserts that:

Thousands are, to use their own words, "resting on John 3:16," or 5:24, and have not the slightest doubt they will spend eternity with Christ. Nevertheless it is the bounden duty of every real servant of God to tell the great majority of them that they are woefully deluded by Satan.[58]

No longer could assurance be found in looking to Christ and His promises alone. Instead, "...the *attainment* of assurance is by an impartial scrutiny of myself and an honest comparing of myself with the scriptural marks of God's children."[59]

It is also interesting to note that, like Augustine, Pink had a fundamental change in his interpretation of Matthew 24:13 after abandoning premillennialism. In *The Redeemer's Return*, Matthew 24:13 is treated as relating to tribulation saints being saved out of the tribulation period through endurance, while in *The Saint's Perseverance*, a work written after his abandonment of premillennialism, Matthew 24:13 is treated as expressing the need for believers to persevere until the end of life in order to be saved eschatologically.[60] As Pink ceased to believe in a literal tribulation period, his interpretation of passages relating to the tribulation necessarily changed as well.

It is not difficult to see that Pink's abandonment of dispensationalism had a profound impact on his soteriology. Such a dramatic change in approach to Biblical interpretation is bound to have an effect on many areas of theology. Soteriology is just one of those areas, but it is one that is impacted as much as any other. The changes in Pink's soteriology when he fundamentally changed his hermeneutics is a case in point.

Conclusion

The debate over Lordship salvation and the debate over dispensationalism are often treated as one and the same. Yet, in recent years, this connection has only been stressed by those who would see both laid to waste. Dispensationalism stands upon the solid ground of a consistent literal interpretation of Scripture and *so does free grace.* It is essential that we in the grace community recognize this connection and understand that as normative dispensationalism is under attack, the foundation upon which free grace stands is being attacked as well.

The rise of dispensationalism in the 19th and 20th centuries brought with it a revival of the principles of grace. It is not coincidence that as the allegorizing of men was replaced by the unadulterated clarity of God's Word, the legalism of men was also replaced by the free grace of God. The nature of man is invariably legalistic, while God is unendingly gracious.

Furthermore, if it can be demonstrated conclusively that Lordship salvation is dependent upon a non-literal approach to portions of Scripture, the shaky ground upon which Lordship salvation stands is exposed. At the face of it, this seems like it may be a difficult task, but this is being plainly admitted by many proponents of Lordship salvation as they eschew dispensationalism. This is further evidenced in the application of non-literal hermeneutics among Lordship salvation proponents in their discussions on soteriology, as will be demonstrated in the next chapter.

CHAPTER 2

Lordship Salvation:
How They Get There

Introduction

Three major distinctions of covenant theology most often drive the soteriology of Lordship salvation. These are kingdom-now millennial views (including already/not yet views), a soteriological view of history, and the application of the law to Christians, all of which are the fruit of non-literal interpretation.

Hermeneutical Differences

While both sides of the debate over dispensationalism agree that dispensationalism and consistent literal interpretation necessarily go together, some have sought to cast doubt on the motivation behind dispensationalists' insistence on consistent literal interpretation. For example, in both *A Primer on Dispensationalism*[61] and *Wrongly Dividing the Word of Truth*,[62] Gerstner makes the claim that theology drives dispensationalism to consistent literal interpretation,[63] rather than consistent literal interpretation driving dispensational theology. This is a strange assertion. It is unlikely that an interpreter would construct a theology independent of Scripture that is coincidentally the same as what the Biblical authors intended to communicate. Scripture is revelation by necessity. That is, its contents are available to us only because God has revealed them, and they are beyond the scope of our imagination.

The fact that literal hermeneutics is indeed primary for dispensationalists is further evidenced in the fact that, while dispensationalists disagree on many theological points, and even on the interpretation of many passages, the commitment to consistent literal interpretation remains. Some of these different approaches, as they relate to the Sermon on the Mount, are cataloged in John Martin's article, "Dispensational Approaches to the Sermon on the Mount" in *Essays in Honor of J. Dwight Pentecost*,[64] and this list is far from exhaustive. The Sermon on the Mount is only one of many passages in which dispensationalists disagree, yet it is fair to say that all of the views arise out of an attempt to uncover the sermon's original intention.

Because dispensationalism is variously defined, I attempted to boil down the five basic elements of normative dispensationalism in the first chapter. A review of these points will be helpful here:

1. Literal, historical, grammatical interpretation should be applied to *all* portions of Scripture.

2. The church and Israel are distinct peoples in God's program for the ages.

3. The Lord Jesus Christ will return bodily to earth and reign on David's throne in Jerusalem for 1,000 years.

4. The underlying purpose of God's dealings with the world is His glory, not merely the salvation of man; thus, the Scripture goes far beyond evangelism.

5. The Christian is free from the law in its entirety for both justification (Gal 2:16) and sanctification (Gal 5:18).[65]

Each of these points is fundamental to normative dispensationalism, but the first point is primary among them because all of the other points flow from consistent literal interpretation.

It is commonly taken as axiomatic that conservative proponents of covenant theology only adopt a method of non-literal interpretation in passages related to yet-unfulfilled prophecy. This is simply not true, as can be seen in the fact that so often the debate between methods of interpretation between dispensationalists and non-dispensationalists focuses on passages that are not prophetical. Some obvious examples are the Sermon on the Mount,[66] Romans 6 to 8, the warning passages in Hebrews[67] and the non-prophetic portions of the Old Testament. If the only divergence is in yet-unfulfilled prophecy, why would passages such as these be the focus of discussion rather than it being limited to books and passages like Daniel 2 and 9, the Olivet Discourse and Revelation?

The fact is, because of the analogy of faith (Scripture interprets Scripture), Bible interpretation is systematic. The theology that arises from our interpretation of one passage necessarily affects our interpretation of other related passages unless we are willing to abandon that theology. The doctrine that arises from non-literal interpretation in eschatological passages produces a domino effect in which non-literal interpretation is adopted in many other passages as well in order to maintain the theology that arises from non-literal interpretation of these passages. By the time the dominoes stop falling, the vast majority of the Bible is impacted and very little is taken in a way that is consistent with authorial intent.

If covenant theology has an impact on the interpretation of so much of the Bible, it should be an area of concern, then, that many dispensational pastors and teachers have bookshelves that are filled primarily with exegetical and theological works from non-dispensational scholars. The mistake is made when assuming that as long as they are not dealing with eschatology, the non-dispensational approach is acceptable. This has caused many dispensationalists to adopt non-dispensational interpretations of many passages and carry away a theology that is inconsistent with a consistently literal approach to Bible interpretation.

MacArthur is only one example of a dispensationalist that has been affected by non-dispensational scholars in this way. This effect can be seen most clearly in his soteriological work, *The Gospel According to Jesus*. In his discussion of the synoptic gospels, he quotes from 39 non-dispensationalists and only one dispensationalist in defense of his position. The effect of this dependence upon non-dispensationalists can be seen in his open rejection of normative dispensationalism in both *The Gospel According to Jesus* and *The Gospel According to the Apostles,* especially (out of our five essentials listed above) the principles of the believer's freedom from the Mosaic Law for both justification and sanctification[68] and dispensationalism's doxological view of history.[69] MacArthur's adoption of the corresponding principles of covenant theology is clearly the foundation for his soteriology.

Millennial Views

Because the impact of the various millennial views upon soteriology has been discussed at length by free grace scholars, this topic will only be dealt with briefly in this work.

While every major aspect of covenant theology has a significant impact on soteriology, nothing has more of an impact than removing the judgment seat of Christ from the equation—a byproduct of kingdom-now millennial views. Dave Anderson writes in *Free Grace Soteriology*:

> Free Grace is an outflow of Dispensationalism. Only Dispensationalism has a judgment seat for believers some time before the thousand year reign of Christ (in Jerusalem on earth) and a judgment seat for unbelievers after this one thousand year reign.[70]

The judgment seat of Christ is a watershed doctrine in soteriology.

There are clearly passages in the New Testament—lots of them—that speak of a judgment of believers according to works. One unambiguous example is 2 Corinthians 5:10: "For we must all appear before the judgment seat of Christ, that each one may receive the things done in the body, according to what he has done, whether good or bad." But there are also many passages that simply talk about rewards in the kingdom according to works without mentioning a judgment. The Beatitudes in Matthew 5:3-12 offer an example of one such passage. For the dispensationalist, these passages present no problem because we understand that there is a judgment for believers to determine reward which is not to be confused with a general judgment of all men to determine eternal destiny.

When the millennial kingdom is removed from the equation—and the judgment seat of Christ with it—the non-dispensationalist is presented with a difficult problem. Passages discussing kingdom inheritance (which is according to works) are equated with passages about the new birth (which is by grace through faith and apart from works). Furthermore, the judgments of unbelievers and believers are joined into one event, one judgment, to determine eternal destiny.[71] If justification and eternal life are a free gift through faith alone apart from works, how can so many passages speak as if kingdom inheritance (which, in their mind, is the same thing[72]) is according to works? And how can believers be judged by their works alongside unbelievers to determine eternal destiny?

Proponents of various forms of Lordship salvation seek to solve this problem by denying the dichotomy set forth in Romans 4:1-5 and 11:6 and reintroducing commitment to good works as either an open condition for finally escaping eternal condemnation or as the necessary outcome of the new birth.[73]

One aspect that is less often discussed is regarding the Biblical description of the righteous life of Israel in the kingdom. For example, Zephaniah 3:11-13 says:

> In that day you shall not be shamed for any of your deeds
> In which you transgress against Me;
> For then I will take away from your midst
> Those who rejoice in your pride,
> And you shall no longer be haughty
> In My holy mountain.
> I will leave in your midst
> A meek and humble people,
> And they shall trust in the name of the LORD.
> The remnant of Israel shall do no unrighteousness
> And speak no lies,
> Nor shall a deceitful tongue be found in their mouth;
> For they shall feed *their* flocks and lie down,
> And no one shall make *them* afraid.

Under covenant theology, the church and Israel are equated and the kingdom is said (at least to some degree) to be in place now. If this is the case, the certain expectation is that all believers must meet this (practically) righteous description.[74] The fact that this is observably removed from reality has led covenant theologians to apply the *No True Scotsman* fallacy[75] to this situation. That is, when it can be observed that believers in Christ do not always meet this practically righteous description, they assert that no *true* believer can fail to live up to it, thus, their assertion becomes unfalsifiable. One problem that this fallacy creates is that it becomes impossible to determine whether or not anyone is a *true* believer, even ourselves, since true belief is only said to be validated by a lifetime of good works. Even if I am doing good works now, how do I know what the future holds for me?

Soteriological View of History

Related to the various kingdom-now views is covenant theology's soteriological view of history. One prevalent theme that ties the entire Bible together is the hope of a future kingdom ruled by the Messiah along with the glory of the Lord that will be both revealed and shared with men during His righteous reign. Because the millennial kingdom is either greatly minimized or eliminated altogether in the various non-dispensational views, an enormous vacuum is left. Scholars have attempted to fill this void by placing redemption of unconditionally elected people at the forefront and reading much of the Bible through that perspective. In that regard, the departure from literal interpretation of passages related to the kingdom is the root of the soteriological view of history.

It might also be said, however, that covenant theology's sote-riological view of history has its roots in the Reformed view of election and reprobation, especially in supralapsarianism.[76] This is best illustrated by William Perkins, who synthesized the theologies of Theodore Beza and the Heidelberg Theologians[77] (the innovators of covenant theology) in his chart of history entitled *A Golden Chaine*.[78] This work was enormously popular and had a profound impact on Puritan theology.

Perkins saw human history as a means of working out election and reprobation. In *A Golden Chaine*, every major Biblical event, along with the lives of both the elect and the reprobate, are mapped from eternity past to eternity future, and each event is seen as a step in the outworking of God's decreed will concerning election and reprobation. In this perspective, all of history is seen as Divinely designed toward those particular goals. While supralapsarianism has become a less common position, the soteriological view of history that resulted from it has remained as popular as ever. A soteriological view of history brings with it an almost exclusively soteriological view of the Bible's contents because everything else is seen as nearly superfluous.

For example, in Piper's *The Justification of God*, he bases his exegesis of Romans 9:1-23 upon the assumption that Israel's position as recipients of God's kingdom program is not the subject of discussion. His comments on Romans 9:2 demonstrate this perspective: "Paul is not moved to constant grief (9:2) because corporate Israel has forfeited her non-salvific 'theocratic privileges' while another people (the church or the remnant) has taken over this 'historical role.'"[79] This implies that it is ridiculous to think Paul

would be so upset about this; however, if we have a proper apprecia-
tion for the importance of the kingdom in God's program for the
ages (see Rom. 8:17-18), and especially the centrality of the kingdom
in God's program for Israel, this notion is not so ridiculous. By
forfeiting their kingdom inheritance, this disobedient generation
is forfeiting its purpose and glory.

A doxological view of God's dealing with man in history, as
opposed to a soteriological view, is to some degree the direct result
of recognizing the intended audience of the Biblical books. If indeed
the only book of the New Testament that was written to unbelievers is
the gospel of John, why would we assume an evangelical purpose for
the other books? Is this not a complete dismissal of authorial intent?

In Edmund K. Neufeld's June 2008 *JETS* article, "The Gospel
in the Gospels: Answering the Question 'What Must I Do to be
Saved?' from the Synoptics," the error of covenant theology's soteriological view of history is on display. Neufeld states that he "will not
contend with the common view that the Synoptic Gospels address
believers, in Matthew's case Jewish believers."[80] Nevertheless he
proceeds to "examine Matthew, Mark, and Luke, reading each
Gospel in turn through the eyes of its own hypothetical reader"
each of which is "a late first-century Gentile unbeliever."[81] This
seems to be an admission that his interpretation is dependent
upon superimposing an audience that was never intended onto
the books in question.

The impact of this error cannot be overstated. Throughout
the article, Neufeld openly and repeatedly states that works are a

condition for receiving eternal life.[82] In fact, this seems to be the main point of the article, as the following thesis paragraph shows:

> . . . we have understood saving *faith* to emerge from God's call and merit-less human choice, so we should understand saving *obedience* rising from that same dynamic of God's grace and merit-less human response. Perhaps the crucial distinction is not between faith and works, but between grace and merit. By saying "faith not works," we intend "grace not merit," but these are not parallel distinctions. The Synoptics undermine "faith not works," but they support "grace not merit."[83]

The intended audience and purpose of any book are inseparably linked. If Matthew was writing to Jewish believers who already possessed eternal life in the Johannine sense, why would he write to them as if they were unbelieving Gentiles who did not already possess this gift? To create a hypothetical reader that is different in every significant way from the intended audience is to skew the intention of the author. Neufeld has simply ignored the intended audience and has imposed an evangelistic purpose onto the text.[84]

Neufeld's plain admission of this method and resulting works salvation is helpful because it brings out into the open a method—rooted in covenant theology's soteriological view of history—that is commonplace among proponents of Lordship salvation.

Is this a fault of Neufeld's exegesis alone, or is it the natural result of covenant theology? I think it is the latter. Covenant theology unites all of Scripture around the doctrine of soteriology. This naturally results in the synoptic gospels playing a central role in the development of its soteriology because soteriology is seen as almost the single purpose of Christ's first advent. If we limit the synoptics' application to people who are already secure believers, while also recognizing the dispensational distinctions that are at play, soteriology ceases to be relevant to their main purpose. Covenant theology (which unites all Scripture around soteriology) simply does not know what to do with a non-soteriological purpose because, in its view, nothing else is truly very important.[85] In Neufeld's article, as in others, changing each synoptic gospel's audience in order to change their purpose seems to be as much about restoring relevance (and even a primary place) to the synoptics as it is about defending a prior commitment to works salvation.

MacArthur also applies this non-literal method of interpretation, as can be plainly seen in his discussion of the purpose of the gospels:

> There is no more glorious truth in the Bible than the words of Luke 19:10: "The Son of Man has come to seek and to save that which was lost." That verse sums up the work of Christ on earth. . . . Unfortunately traditional Dispensationalism tends to miss that simple point. Some Dispensationalists teach that "the gospel of the kingdom" Jesus proclaimed (Matt 4:23) is distinct from "the gospel of the grace of God." . . . That may fit neatly into a particular Dispensational scheme, but Scripture does not support it. We must not forget that Jesus came to seek and save the lost, not merely to announce an earthly kingdom.[86]

This quote misrepresents the dispensational position. Dispensationalists also agree that Jesus proclaimed the way to eternal life—the fourth gospel is dedicated primarily to this purpose (cf. John 20:31). The difference is that normative dispensationalists recognize that Jesus spoke about other things too, whereas MacArthur would force an evangelistic purpose onto all of Jesus' words, no matter the context.[87] Would MacArthur, a premillennialist, have us believe that Jesus did not offer an earthly kingdom at all? His words here and the way he uses passages in which Jesus offers the kingdom to Israel suggest that he would.

John Piper also reveals this perspective in his discussion of what it takes to obtain what he calls "final salvation." After quoting or referencing Matthew 10:37; Mark 8:34-35; Luke 14:33; Acts 3:19; 1 Corinthians 16:22 and many other passages, he goes on to say:

> These are just some of the conditions that the New Testament says we must meet in order to inherit final salvation. We must believe on Jesus and receive him and turn from our sin and obey him and humble ourselves like little children and love him more than we love our family, our possession, or our own life. This is what it means to be converted to Christ. This alone is the way of life everlasting.[88]

This comment shows that he is interpreting all of these passages as being about how to obtain eternal life. He does this even though all of these books were written to believers and none of these passages mention faith, eternal life, justification or eternal condemnation.

Piper's use here of Acts 3:19 is especially telling because the passage is discussing the conditions for bringing in the "times of refreshing" and "the times of restoration of all things" (Acts 3:21) which were foretold by the Old Testament prophets (cf. Acts 3:22-24) and are clearly a reference to the kingdom.[89] Though Piper holds to covenant theology, he is premillennial in his eschatology and should not have missed this.[90]

Though Biblical writers can (and sometimes do) discuss the way to eternal life in books written to believers, this is done as a reminder and as a foundation for other doctrines.[91] Because the audience of every book in the New Testament other than the gospel of John is an audience of believers, we should not assume that every serious discussion in the Bible is about the eternal destiny of its readers; but that is exactly what non-dispensationalists often do. The covenant theologian and the *leaky dispensationalist* (MacArthur) find their justification for this assumption in their soteriological view of history and, in MacArthur's case, the over-application of Luke 19:10. Non-soteriological passages thus form the foundation of the soteriology of Lordship salvation proponents, and this ultimately results in confusion regarding the condition for spending eternity with God.

The Mosaic Law

The intermingling of law and grace that is common (though not universal[92]) among those who reject normative dispensationalism is the result of the continuity principle of covenant theology (which progressive dispensationalism has also adopted). While Daniel Fuller disagrees with the dispensationalist position, he sums up the dispensationalist's argument on this point well:

> Dispensationalism is convinced that covenant theology is unable to keep law and grace separate because it insists on maintaining a continuity between God's dealings with Israel and with the Church. It argues that covenant theology, in insisting upon this continuity, must mix the law, which characterizes God's dealings with Israel, with the message of grace and the gospel, which is a unique characteristic of God's dealings with the Church.[93]

By prioritizing continuity above literal interpretation, covenant theologians deny the distinction between the church and Israel and seek to give primary application to every portion of the Bible, often including the Mosaic Law. This principle of covenant theology[94] is best illustrated by Arthur Pink in *The Law and the Saint*:

> It is a superficial and erroneous conclusion that supposes the Old and New Testaments are antagonistic. The Old Testament is full of grace: The New Testament is full of Law. The revelation of the New Testament to the Old is like that of the oak tree to the acorn. It has been often said, and said truly, "The New is in the Old contained, the Old is by the New explained"! And surely this *must be* so. The Bible as a whole, and in its parts, is not merely for Israel or the Church, but is a written revelation from God to and for *the whole human race*.[95]

This quote broadly dismisses the idea that any book of the Bible has a particular audience in mind, since the suggestion is that, "the Bible as a whole, and in its parts" is "to . . . *the whole human race*." This quote is illustrative of the main theme of his book and of covenant theology's application of the law to today.

Though MacArthur claims a form of dispensationalism, he has largely adopted covenant theology's position on the application of the law today, especially as it relates to sanctification. MacArthur does state the Christian's freedom from the law,[96] but he limits this to the freedom from the law's penalties,[97] and often removes the emphasis on freedom from the law in Paul's writings. For example, he treats Romans 7:1-4 as if Paul is discussing freedom from sin, rather than freedom from the law,[98] and places almost no emphasis on freedom from the law in his extended discussion on Romans 6 to 8. In his discussion on Romans 7, he skips verses 5 to 11 entirely and never mentions the fact that the law actually arouses indwelling sin (which is one of the necessary reasons why we are freed from it, and is the main point of Rom. 7; see Rom. 7:5, 9-11). As a result, Romans 7:14-24 is not seen as an abnormal experience for a Christian, or as one Christian's experience when trying to live under the law, but as "the state of every true believer."[99]

This may seem like a small matter soteriologically. It is about sanctification after all. But dispensationalism recognizes that the freedom from sin described in Romans 6 to 8, Galatians 2:19-5:23 and elsewhere *is conditioned upon the Christian realizing his freedom from the law* (see esp. Rom 6:14; 7:5-6; and Gal 2:19-21). And when that condition is removed or minimized, the freedom from sin it describes can be presented as if it were a discussion of what it means to be a true Christian. This is precisely what MacArthur and many other Lordship salvation proponents do.

By applying the law to Christians for sanctification, the passages in the Bible that discuss freedom from the law in regards to sanctification are twisted into discussions about proof of justification. This can be clearly seen in one of MacArthur's books on soteriology, *The Gospel According to the Apostles*, in which Romans 6 to 8, which comes *after* the Apostle Paul considered the issue of his readers' justification to be settled (see 5:1) and is entirely about sanctification (6:1–8:15) and glorification (8:16-39), receives two whole chapters of discussion (chaps. 7-8). This is more attention than any other Biblical passage. Once again, non-soteriological passages form the basis for the soteriology of Lordship salvation. This is no less true in passages discussing freedom from the law than it is in passages discussing the millennial kingdom or other non-soteriological issues. Recognizing the Christian's freedom from the law for justification and sanctification is vital to both literal interpretation and correct soteriology, just as it is vital for sanctification itself.

Conclusion

All conservative Bible interpreters believe in literal interpretation, but only the dispensationalist applies this consistently. But because Bible interpretation is systematic, non-literal interpretation in one area necessarily affects other areas as well. Each of the four theological points of dispensationalism discussed in this chapter (points 2-5) is a means to protect the first point: consistent literal interpretation. When any of those points are abandoned or minimized,[100] the interpreter inevitably steps away from consistent literal interpretation—and consistent literal interpretation is the only way to maintain a Biblical soteriology.

Denying a literal millennial kingdom confuses the judgment seat of Christ with the great white throne judgment and brings in a final judgment for believers according to works to determine eternal destiny. Having a soteriological view of history rather than a doxological one leads to interpreting non-soteriological passages soteriologically and confuses the conditions for spending eternity with God. Finally, placing the Christian under the law removes realization of Christian freedom as a condition for a holy walk and thus makes a holy walk the necessary outcome of the new birth. These are just some of the areas in which departing from dispensationalism results in confusion about what it takes to have eternal life.

CHAPTER 3

The Fruit of Dispensationalism

Introduction

While covenant theology most naturally leads to Lordship salvation, dispensationalism most naturally leads to free grace theology. This chapter covers, first, the historical linkage[101] between dispensationalism and free grace; second, the theological linkage; and third, some practical applications for those who hold to both dispensationalism and free grace.

Dispensationalism and Free Grace: Historically Linked

MacArthur has argued that free grace theology finds its roots in Chafer's dispensationalism.[102] It is fair to say that Chafer, with the founding of Dallas Theological Seminary and with the writing of *He That Is Spiritual*,[103] *Grace: An Exposition of God's Marvelous Gift*[104] and his *Systematic Theology*,[105] had a profound impact on the development of free grace theology. It is also true, however, that as dispensationalism predates him in English and American theology, so does free grace. Because this topic could fill volumes, the free grace writings of the early dispensationalists will be only briefly surveyed.

Dispensationalism arose from Calvinistic theologians. The Brethren dispensationalists such as J. N. Darby, C. H. Mackintosh and William Kelley, and the Presbyterian and Congregationalist dispensationalists such as James Hall Brookes, C. I. Scofield, and Chafer were all Calvinists of a sort, though the idea of limited atonement was not apparently held by any of them. Despite this, they did not entirely break from Calvinism and all held to a soft view of the perseverance of the saints, namely that all true believers would have at least some change and works in their lives.

But in addition to dispensationalism itself, two significant developments came through these dispensational Calvinists. First, they brought to the forefront doctrines other than soteriology, especially eschatology and ecclesiology. Second, they adamantly warned against looking to works for assurance.[106]

Another benefit of this survey of the soteriology of historical dispensationalists is that it answers the charge that free grace is a modern creation borne out of a backlash against the Lordship salvation of MacArthur and others. It will be demonstrated that systematized free grace theology is at least as old as systematized dispensationalism.

Bringing to the Forefront Doctrines Other Than Soteriology

Regarding the first point, Mackintosh's short essay, "Calvinism and Arminianism: One Sided Theology" is representative of the dispensational sentiment of his day. In it, he argues that while he believes the five points of Calvinism to be true, they by no means consist of the whole counsel of God. He writes:

> We believe these five points, so far as they go;[107] but they are very far indeed from containing the faith of God's elect. There are wide fields of divine revelation which this stunted and one-sided system does not touch upon, or even hint at, in the most remote manner. Where do we find the heavenly calling? Where, the precious sanctifying hope of the coming of Christ to receive His people to Himself? Where have we the grand scope of prophecy opened to the vision of our souls, in that which is so pompously styled "the faith of God's elect"?[108]

Mackintosh further observes that obsession with the doctrines of Calvinism (or with Arminianism for that matter) leads to a stunted spirituality:

> Nothing is more damaging to the truth of God, more withering to the soul, or more subversive of all spiritual growth and progress than mere theology, high or low—Calvinistic or Arminian. It is impossible for the soul to make progress

beyond the boundaries of the system to which it is attached. If I am taught to regard "the five points" as "the faith of God's elect," I shall not think of looking beyond them; and then a most glorious field of heavenly truth is shut out from the vision of my soul. I am stunted, narrowed, one-sided; and I am in danger of getting into that hard, dry state of soul which results from being occupied with mere points of doctrine instead of with Christ.[109]

While Mackintosh is not directly commenting on covenant theology's soteriological view of history, the fact that he had broken free from it gave him the perspective to properly place soteriology in its rightful place as one of many glorious doctrines expressed in Scripture. As I argued in chapter two, this lays the foundation for rightly interpreting large portions of the Bible as non-soteriological and paves the way for distinguishing justification from sanctification and the free gift from reward.[110]

Assurance Without Introspection

In sharp contrast to the non-dispensationalists, the belief that assurance should be found in looking to Christ and His promises alone rather than to works was almost universally held among the early dispensationalists. And some of them argued vigorously for it. Some extended quotes are necessary to demonstrate how forcefully these dispensationalists expounded this belief.

Darby presented faith and the peace (assurance) which it brings as properly resting on God's Word, not on experience:

In real communion the conscience must be purged; there can be no communion if the soul be not at peace. We read here, "By one offering he hath perfected forever them that are sanctified." There is very frequently the confounding of what faith produces with what faith rests upon. Faith always rests upon God's estimate of the blood of Jesus as He has revealed it in His word: faith rests on no experience.[111]

Mackintosh takes this further, arguing that looking to works for assurance is not even Christianity:

The Spirit of God never leads any one to build upon His work as the ground of peace, but only upon the finished work of Christ, and the unchangeable word of God; and we may rest assured that the more simply we rest on these the more settled our peace will be, and the clearer our evidences, the brighter our frames, the happier our feelings, the richer our experiences.

In short, the more we look away from self and all its belongings, and rest in Christ, on the clear authority of scripture, the more spiritually minded we shall be; and the inspired apostle tells us that "to be spiritually minded (or, the minding of the Spirit) is life and peace." The best evidence of a spiritual mind is child-like repose in Christ and His word. The clearest proof of an unspiritual mind is self-occupation. It is a poor affair to be trafficking in *our* evidences, or *our* anything. It looks like piety, but it leads away from Christ—away from scripture—away from God; and this is not piety, or faith, or Christianity.[112]

Thus, from the earliest days of systematized dispensationalism, a free grace view of assurance was already strongly represented and had near universal acceptance. This is continued by dispensational-ists even today.

James Hall Brookes, who has been called the "father of American dispensationalism,"[113] makes perhaps an even more robust defense of the freeness of eternal life and assurance through Christ's promises alone. His work, *Salvation: The Way Made Plain*, devotes 362 pages to the topic[114] (the rest of the book expresses the impossibility of man earning salvation through works) and argues for the believer's right to absolute assurance apart from works from many different angles. For example:

> It is my earnest desire and effort to turn your thoughts entirely away from yourself to the Saviour, for it is the most melancholy business that can engage even a redeemed sin-ner to be probing into his own soul to find some assurance that he is saved. You can never find it there, but only in the word; and, thank God! having once seen it in the word, you can see it every day and every hour, and as often as you read and believe what Jesus says. Nor is this assurance the privilege exclusively of ministers or of a favoured few who have made higher attainments in holiness than the common crowd can ever hope to reach, but it is the privilege of every one without exception who believes the testimony of God's word addressed alike to all.[115]

Illustrating the distinctiveness of the dispensational posi-tion on this issue, Brookes commented on the profound difference between the lack of assurance that was prevalent in his day and what he saw in the New Testament:

[T]here is abundant proof that [the believers to whom the NT epistles were written] were strangers to the fear and uncertainty that make up the gloomy experience of at least nine-tenths of the people of God in modern times. Whoever they were, whatever they had been, wherever they lived, they had an assurance of salvation which must have formed at once an unfailing fountain of joy to their hearts and an effective instrument for achieving an easy victory over the world.[116]

Examples such as these could be multiplied in this work. Likewise, other early dispensationalists, Robert Govett,[117] C. I. Scofield,[118] D. M. Panton[119] and, to a lesser extent, William Kelly[120] shared this view. The near uniformity on this issue among dispensationalists is especially noteworthy because dispensationalism spread as a grassroots movement, mostly in independent churches, and without a top-down structure. Even those who might be styled leaders of the movement, rather than developing creeds and confessions, implored everyone to look only to Scripture to determine truth. For example, Darby says:

This is what I would press and urge upon every one: to apply themselves, for themselves, to the testimony of Scripture, to draw ideas simply and directly from this (and I can assure them, they will ever find them sanctifying ideas) but trust no man's mind, whether millenarian or amillenarian.[121]

The Larger Theological Landscape

Historically, dispensationalism has been essentially free grace from the beginning. The scope of this work does not permit a full treatment of the soteriology of the popular non-dispensationalists of the 19th century. However, in order to show the sharp contrast between it and the soteriology of these dispensationalists, I have included a few quotes from some of the most popular 19th-century theologians.

In his most well-known work, *Holiness*, J. C. Ryle (who today might be considered a *leaky dispensationalist*) writes:

> We must be holy, because this is the *only sound evidence that we have a saving faith in our Lord Jesus Christ.* . . . True faith will always show itself by fruits,—it will sanctify, it will work by love, it will overcome the world, it will purify the heart.[122]

Similarly, Charles Hodge contends:

> . . . it is only a living faith, *i.e.*, a faith which works by love and purifies he heart, that unites the soul to Christ and secures our reconciliation with God. . . . No man is delivered from the guilt of sin who is not delivered from its reigning power . . . sanctification is inseparable from justification, and . . . one is just as essential as the other.[123]

Finally, in a paper written against the Plymouth Brethren (who were dispensationalists), Robert L. Dabney wrote in favor of looking for assurance by subjectively looking to our own works rather than objectively looking to Christ:

... we find the apostle expressly *commanding* Christians to seek their assurance of being in Christ, partly in that very way which these writers condemn as legalism and the very antithesis of faith. ... We find the Bible saints testing the nature of their faith and their title to a union with Christ, by their subjective affections and principles. ... James ii. 20: "Faith without works is dead." The laying down of these marks evidently implies that believers are to apply them to themselves ; [*sic*] and by that means, rationally, scripturally and spiritually ascertain the spuriousness or genuineness of their union to Christ. ... The truth is, that not only faith, but love, filial obedience, true repentance, Christian patience, forgiveness, (see Galatians v. 22, 23,) etc., are fruits, and so *marks*, of God's sovereign new birth in the soul.[124]

Many more such examples could be provided, but these must suffice. The inseparability of justification and sanctification, and thus, the impossibility of absolute assurance based on faith alone, was taken as a given by the larger theological community. It was in the midst of legalistic gloom that dispensationalism provided a floodlight of grace and assurance to all who had eyes to see.

A Revival of Grace

Chafer did not alone revive free grace theology. He merely picked up where the dispensationalists before him had left off and increased its popularity through his writings and the establishment of Dallas Theological Seminary.

The view expressed earlier in quotes by Mackintosh and

Brookes that assurance is the foundation of a holy walk was also the cornerstone of Chafer's teaching on the spiritual life. For example, in the first lesson of his series of lectures on the Christian Life addressed to DTS students, Chafer said:

> Now honestly look into your heart. Has that been the motive in your Christian life, that you have lived the best you could because you were set right, or did you live the best you could hoping to be set right? There is a world of difference between those two things. I am sure that you don't need for me to multiply words here. But that is the difference right on the basis of it of law and grace and you're not under law because law in that system cannot apply or cannot enter into your relation to God at the present time. You would be insulting Him. You can see, I'm sure, you'd be insulting Him to immediately try to put yourself on an earn basis and as you put yourself there to say, "well I'll add something to what God has done" and what He has done is to give me the perfection. I am perfect in it forever in the one sacrifice of Christ. I *am* that. Now I *am* that.[125]

This concept is presented as foundational to the whole series of lectures.

DTS, founded by Dr. Chafer, was the alma mater of Charles Ryrie, Zane Hodges, Earl Radmacher, Bob Wilkin, Charles Bing, Joseph Dillow, Dwight Pentecost, Roy Zuck, Elliott Johnson, and others who have consistently and powerfully expounded and defended free grace from a dispensational perspective.

Dispensationalism and Free Grace: Theologically Linked

The connection between dispensationalism and free grace is not merely historical, it is theological as well. In the following section I lay out a few of these connections.

Purpose for National Israel

What does God do with His children who are stiff-necked and rebellious? Does His holiness demand they be cast aside, or does His great integrity ensure that His promises stand firm, despite the rebellion of His people? The way we answer this question profoundly influences our view of God, of grace, and the security of the believer. With respect to Israel, dispensationalists and non-dispensationalists cannot offer the same answer to this question. Dispensationalists, taking a consistent literal view of Scripture, view God as faithful to His promises to Israel despite their disobedience while non-dispensationalists allegorize these promises and view God as casting national Israel aside to be replaced by the church.

After the first four centuries of the church, and prior to the systemization of dispensationalism by Darby (around 1828), Christendom almost universally believed that God had cast aside national Israel, visiting upon them all of the curses of the Mosaic Covenant. Likewise, they reserved in their minds all of the blessings of the Abrahamic, Mosaic, Davidic and New Covenants exclusively for the church. This is still the case for non-dispensationalists today.

As Bell states, covenant (or federal) theology casts its over-arching idea of the covenant of grace in a light of conditionality:

> In this covenant, God promised eternal life to the elect on the condition of acting faith in Jesus Christ. . . . By insert-ing the element of conditionality into the arena of grace, the Federalists frequently distorted the nature of grace and faith. In the covenantal theology, grace too often ceased to be the unconditional expression of God's love for his people, and became, in the mercantile language of the Federalists, a commodity purchased by man in God's marketplace.[126]

Thus, in their view, man purchased and maintained cove-nantal relationship through active (working) faith.[127] This seems to be the natural result of the view that God has abandoned Israel despite His promises to them. If failure to persevere in obedience released God from His promises to Israel, why not also the ones made to the individual believer? In the view of covenant theology, both are related to the same *covenant of grace*, so if one is breakable, the other must be as well.

By contrast, the dispensationalist sees several covenants of a different nature. The Mosaic Covenant *was* wholly conditional (more on this below). Under it, Israel was promised blessing for obedience and cursing if they were disobedient. The Mosaic Covenant was breakable and indeed was broken. But, the Abrahamic, Davidic, and New Covenants[128] are guaranteed by God's faithfulness alone and cannot be broken. In the forging of the Abrahamic Covenant, God alone passed between the hewn animals, demonstrating that

He alone is responsible for seeing that it comes to pass (Gen 15:8-17). The Davidic and New Covenants, which further refine the Abrahamic,[129] are no less breakable.

Because of this understanding of the covenants, dispensationalists see that, despite Israel's disobedience, God has not entirely cast them aside, and that He still has a plan for their national redemption upon Christ's return. While the church is grafted into Abraham's blessing, it does not supplant Israel and God will not under any circumstance allow His covenant to fail (see Ps. 89:20-37; Jer. 33:19-20; Ezek. 37).

One can easily see that this naturally supports the free grace position. On the front end, faith (active or otherwise) is not a means by which we purchase a covenant relationship; it is merely the channel by which God imparts the free gift of everlasting life.[130] Likewise, the security of the believer echoes God's dealings with Israel in the Abrahamic, Davidic and New Covenants, in that those who have received everlasting life by faith are entirely in God's hands and their security is not in any way dependent upon their perseverance. God's faithfulness alone secures Israel's future; and His faithfulness alone ensures the security of eternal life for those who believe in Jesus.

> If we are faithless,
> He remains faithful;
> He cannot deny Himself. (2 Tim. 2:13)

Mosaic Law and the Christian

Everything in the Mosaic Law is conditioned upon works of obedience. This is plainly declared in Leviticus 18:5, "You shall therefore keep My statutes and My judgments, which if a man does, he shall live by them: I *am* the LORD" (see also Deut. 28).[131] The Apostle Paul picks up on this and expresses the contrast between works-righteousness through the law on the one hand and imputed righteousness through faith on the other in Galatians 3:1-14 and elsewhere.

As discussed in the previous chapter, dispensationalism alone is able to consistently maintain the distinction between grace and the law, and failing to do so introduces an element of conditionality into the relationship between the Savior and the Christian. However, in keeping the church distinct from Israel and the Mosaic dispensation separate from the dispensation of grace, the dispensationalist is able to decisively and finally sever the ties between the Christian and the Mosaic Law as emphatically asserted by the Apostle Paul (Rom. 6:14; 7:4-6; 2 Cor. 3:3-18; Gal. 2:16-3:25; 4:4-5; Eph. 2:14-16; Col. 2:11-23, etc.). This was the case among dispensationalists from the very beginning. Commenting on Romans 7, Darby writes: ". . . we cannot be at the same time under the law and with Christ risen. This would be to have two husbands at once."[132]

McClain sums up the dispensationalist position on the believer's freedom from the law in justification, sanctification and preservation:

In Romans 3:20 we read that "by the deeds of the law . . . shall no flesh be justified in his sight." And in this text the Holy Spirit seems to broaden sweepingly the exclusion of all deeds of the law from the divine act in the justification of sinners. There are no definite articles. The Greek text reads simply "by deeds of law." Again in Romans 6:14 the Scripture declares not only that the law as law has absolutely nothing to contribute in the accomplishment of the believer's sanctification, but on the contrary that freedom from the law's bondage is actually one indispensable factor in that important work of God in the soul. Still further, when Paul comes to deal with the matter of Christian security in Romans 8, he asserts that the law has no power to keep us in safety, but "what the law could not do" in this regard, God sent His Son to accomplish for us and also in us (Rom 8:3-4). Thus we see that the law can neither justify, sanctify nor preserve us.[133]

Dispensationalism not only sees the principles of law and grace as mutually exclusive (as means of obtaining the same thing), it sees them as *destructive* to one another. For example, Chafer writes:

The principles of law and grace are mutually destructive, and doctrinal confusion follows the intrusion of any legal principle into the reign of grace. When law is thus intruded, not only is the clear responsibility of the believer under grace obscured, but the priceless attitude of God in grace, which He purchased at the infinite cost of the death of His Son, is wholly misrepresented.[134]

Bringing in the law as a condition for sanctification does not necessarily wipe out justification by faith apart from works entirely, but when it is coupled with the trading and purchasing concept of faith that is found in covenant theology, keeping the law becomes a condition for so-called "final salvation."[135] Thus, by helping the interpreter avoid the pitfall of mixing law and grace, dispensationalism again naturally leads the interpreter to free grace.

Judgment Seat of Christ

Of course, there *is* an element of conditionality (though, not the Mosaic Law) found in Scripture that is primarily addressed to Christians (see, for example: John 15:1-6; Rom. 8:17; 1 Cor. 3:11-15; Phil. 2:12; 2 Pet. 1:5-11). This conditionality is not, however, associated with justification or with a so-called "final salvation." It is related, first, to experiencing fellowship with God (John 14:21; 1 John 1:7). Second, we find it in connection with the judgment seat of Christ where believers will be rewarded for their works. "The judgment seat of Christ" (2 Cor. 5:10), as distinct from the "great white throne" judgment of Revelation 20:11-15, is a concept that is unique to dispensationalism.

The judgment seat of Christ became a primary doctrine early in the development of dispensationalism through British dispensationalist Robert Govett, and was carried on by those he influenced; however, it did not come into the forefront in American free grace theology until Zane Hodges.

Following the publication of *The Hungry Inherit*,[136] the judgment seat of Christ became a staple in free grace literature—and rightly so. While the judgment seat of Christ maintains its prominent place, a free grace interpretation of Scripture is almost inevitable. In addition, the apparent (though not actual) tension in Scripture between faith and works disappears. Faith alone has its proper place and works have theirs. The calls to persevere in order to inherit the kingdom, which are prevalent in the New Testament, are also easily explained without compromising the freeness of everlasting life, undermining the security of the believer or manipulating statements which are clearly conditional into expressing inevitabilities.

Lastly, the doctrine also powerfully answers the charge of antinomianism that is often leveled at free grace. Far from being unimportant, perseverance in faith and good works is tangibly related to the believer's level of enjoyment of eternity because believers are rewarded on the basis of that perseverance (1 Cor. 3:9-15; 2 Cor. 5:10; Rev. 22:12).

EPILOGUE

Conclusion and Practical Applications

Free grace rises and falls with dispensationalism. There have been many teachers in history who have taught free grace without ascribing to dispensationalism. John 3:16 is understandable by anyone who desires to understand it. But such teachers have never represented a large portion of pastors, theologians or other ministers outside of dispensational circles. There are simply too many things that can easily confuse the gospel when the practice of consistent literal hermeneutics is abandoned. But as all of these difficulties are easily answered by dispensationalism, the Bible interpreter who holds to dispensationalism has the liberty to take verses like John 3:16, as well as the many other calls to believe and receive eternal life as a free gift, at face value.

For those who agree with both dispensationalism and free grace, and who recognize the significant connection between the two, some practical applications follow.

Be vocal in sharing dispensationalism. This may seem

like a daunting task, but in most cases, you will not need to walk people through a textbook. Simply pointing out one clear distinction between the church and Israel, between the kingdom and the church, or between law and grace, can go a long way in helping people understand the Scriptures and the grace they teach more clearly. Most people have not heard of these distinctions, and they can certainly be eye-openers. In my experience, I have found that a simple statement about these things can easily turn into an evening full of fruitful conversation.

Teach dispensationalism and hermeneutics in your church when appropriate. This is one of the best ways to prepare disciple-makers. Our church has dispensationalism and hermeneutics as part of our basic discipleship curriculum that our church family goes through.[137] As we have engaged in studying hermeneutics and dispensationalism, our congregation has found a restored interest in Bible study due to greater confidence in being able to understand Scripture, a renewed passion for grace due to seeing it more clearly in Scripture, a growth in the number of volunteers starting new Bible studies with their friends and an increase in evangelism due to greater confidence in being able to field objections. Lastly, as our congregation has become more actively engaged in ministry and more aware of our place in God's immutable plan, we have experienced a greater unity and love for one another.

Because of the terminology, hermeneutics and dispensationalism may sound like dry topics, but they are far from it. Hermeneutics is the tool that equips us to discern the meaning of

God's perfect Word. Dispensationalism is the glorious theme of God's plan for mankind, the thought of which caused the Apostle Paul to burst into beautiful doxologies (cf. Rom. 11:25-36; Eph. 3).

Pray for and support dispensational ministries. If you are unable to teach these topics for one reason or another, you can still pray for and support dispensational ministries. If literal interpretation is not taught to future generations, grace will not be taught to them either. Dispensationalism began as a grassroots movement, and it can continue to be spread at the most basic level. This is because the concepts are simple and because those who embrace these concepts can handle Scripture with confidence. People can share it with their friends and families, and they do not need advanced degrees in order to do so. But even recognizing this, we should still see that laborers are necessary and cheerfully help those who take up this task. The principle laid out by the Lord to the 70 is still true today: "Then He said to them, 'The harvest truly *is* great, but the laborers *are* few; therefore pray the Lord of the harvest to send out laborers into His harvest'" (Luke 10:2).

ENDNOTES

1 "Many people understand John 6:47 as though it read: 'He who whatchamacallits has everlasting life.' Since they don't know what whatchamacallit is, they don't know if they have everlasting life or not." Robert N. Wilkin, "Beware of Confusion about Faith" Journal of the Grace Evangelical Society vol. 18, no. 34 (Spring 2005):3. Wilkin here describes perfectly the confusion I had.

2 *The Message* (Colorado Springs, CO: NavPress Publishing Group, 2002).

3 The Holy Bible, New International Version® (Grand Rapids, MI: Zondervan; Copyright © 1973, 1978, 1984, 2011 by Biblica, Inc.™).

4 This perspective is also in evidence in MacArthur's discussion of early dispensation-alists: "Many of these men were self-taught in theology and were professionals in secular occupations. Darby and Scofield, for example, were attorneys, and Larkin was a mechanical draftsman. They were laymen whose teachings gained enormous popularity largely through grass roots enthusiasm. Unfortunately some of these early framers of dispensationalism were not as precise or discriminating as they might have been had they had the benefit of a more complete theological education." John MacArthur, *The Gospel According to the Apostles* (Nashville: Word Publishing, 2000), p. 223. This is the updated edition of *Faith Works*. Contrast this with Gerstner's assessment of Darby: "John Nelson Darby, for example, was a masterfully knowledgeable man, with expertise in languages and an intimate familiarity with the content of the Bible." John Gerstner, *Wrongly Dividing the Word of Truth: A Critique of Dispensationalism* (Brent-wood, TN: Wolgemuth and Hyatt Publishers Inc., 1991), p. 75. Darby's *capability* as a scholar is not in question, but the fact that he was self-taught is likely to have contributed to him having the freedom to systematize the history of the Bible from the perspective of literal interpretation. Thankfully he was not taught in the allegorical method the seminaries of the time were teaching.

5 C. I. Scofield, *Prophecy Made Plain* (London and Glasgow: Pickering and Inglis Ltd., 1935).

6 Arthur Pink, *A Study of Dispensationalism: And the Ninety-Five Thesis Against Dispensation-alism,* <http://www.pbministries.org/books/pink/Dispensationalism/dispensationalism.

htm>; Internet; accessed 10 February 2011.

7   On one hand, MacArthur states that the link between dispensationalism and free grace is imagined, but on the other he argues later that they are very much linked. I believe that the distinction is that he does not want people to associate all forms of dispensationalism with free grace. Nevertheless, I believe that he would agree that classical or revised dispensationalism in the mold of Chafer or Ryrie (which I have labeled normative dispensationalism) is the root of free grace theology.

8   Spring 2002, 15:29, pp. 25-36; and Autumn, 2002, 15:29, pp. 23-39.

9   There are various views regarding precisely in what way God's glory is central. For my view, see Grant Hawley, *The Guts of Grace: Preparing Ordinary Saints for Extraordinary Ministry* (Allen, TX: Bold Grace Ministries, 2013), pp. 271-81, 335-402.

10   I recognize that as believers, we have the law of Christ to fulfill (Gal. 6:2), but this is a law of liberty (Jas. 1:25; 2:12), fulfilled by love (part of the fruit of the Spirit which is produced in freedom from law; cf. Rom. 13:8, Gal. 5:18-23), and is in contrast to "the law of commandments *contained* in ordinances," which has been "abolished" through Christ's fulfillment of it on the cross (Eph. 2:15; cf. vv. 13-16). "Where the Spirit of the Lord *is*, there is liberty" (2 Cor. 3:17).

11   For points 1-4 see Charles Ryrie, *Dispensationalism* (Chicago: Moody, 2007), pp. 45-48. For point 5, see *The Ryrie Study Bible: New Testament New American Standard Version* (Chicago: Moody, 1977), pp. 273-74 (notes on Rom. 7). See also Alva J. McClain, *Law and Grace: A Study of New Testament Concepts as They Relate to the Christian Life*, (Chicago: Moody, 1991).

12   Ryrie, *Dispensationalism*, pp. 45-48.

13   Progressive dispensationalism adopts a complementary (non-literal) hermeneutic in certain prophetic passages, asserts that Christ is already reigning on David's throne, and denies the distinction between the church and Israel. All are fundamental aspects of dispensationalism. The author recognizes that not all who claim to be progressive dispensationalists would agree with all of these defining qualities of progressive dispensationalism. For more information regarding this stance, see Ryrie, *Dispensationalism*, pp. 189-212.

14   MacArthur's statement about this is not far from accurate: "No covenant theologian defends the no-lordship gospel" (MacArthur, *Apostles*, p. 222).

15   Due to limited space, I will be focusing on the writings of John MacArthur, John Gerstner and Arthur Pink, but the theme of attacking free grace and dispensationalism in the same breath can be seen in the works of John Piper, R.C. Sproul, B.B. Warfield and many others.

16   Whatever the historical argument, surely the burden of proof is upon those who suggest that we should *not* interpret any portion of the Bible literally, respecting the original

intention of the authors.

17 "Dispensationalism is a fundamentally correct system of understanding God's program through the ages. Its chief element is a recognition that God's plan for Israel is not superseded by or swallowed up in His program for the church. Israel and the church are separate entities, and God will restore national Israel under the earthly rule of Jesus as Messiah. I accept and affirm this tenet because it emerges from a consistently literal interpretation of Scripture (while still recognizing the presence of legitimate metaphor in the Bible). And in that regard, I consider myself a traditional premillennial dispensationalist" (John F. MacArthur Jr., *The Gospel According to Jesus*, Revised and Expanded Edition [Grand Rapids: Zondervan, 1988, 1994], p. 31).

18 "It may surprise some readers to know that the issue of dispensationalism is one area where Charles Ryrie, Zane Hodges, and I share some common ground. We are all dispensationalists" (MacArthur, *Apostles*, p. 219).

19 Ibid., p. 221.

20 John Gerstner, *Wrongly Dividing*, pp. 209-63.

21 Reginald Kimbro, *The Gospel According to Dispensationalism* (Toronto: Wittenberg Publications, 1995).

22 See especially pp. 31-35, 96-97, 176-77 and 247-48.

23 The first and second paragraphs of p. 31.

24 See also the following quote from *The Gospel According to the Apostles*, p. 223: "As I have noted, the uniqueness of dispensationalism is that we see a distinction in Scripture between Israel and the church. That *singular* perspective, common to all dispensationalists, sets us apart from non-dispensationalists. It is, by the way, the *only element* of traditional dispensationalist teaching that is yielded as a result of literal interpretation of biblical texts [this claim will be addressed in the next chapter]. It also is the only tenet virtually all dispensationalists hold in common. That is why I have singled it out as the characteristic that defines dispensationalism. When I speak of 'pure' dispensationalism, *I'm referring to this one common denominator*—the Israel-church distinction" (emphasis added).

25 MacArthur, *Jesus*, p. 31.

26 Ibid., p. 96.

27 As the Scripture index of *The Gospel According to Jesus* shows, Luke 19:10 appears more than any other verse outside of the Sermon on the Mount in Matthew and the call to discipleship in Luke 14:26-33. See especially pp. 33, 80, 96 and 103, where MacArthur clearly quotes the verse for the purpose of applying an evangelistic purpose to all of Jesus' teaching.

28 For example, Scofield wrote: "As a dispensation, grace begins with the death and resurrection of Christ (Romans 3:24-26; 4:24-25). The point of testing is no longer legal obedience as the condition of salvation, but acceptance or rejection of Christ" (C. I. Scofield, *Scofield Reference Bible* [New York: Oxford, 1917], p. 1,115). This was clarified in the *New Scofield Bible*, in which it says, "Under the former dispensation, law was shown to be powerless to secure righteousness and life for a sinful race (Gal. 3:21-22). Prior to the cross man's salvation was through faith (Gen. 15:6; Rom. 4:3), being grounded on Christ's atoning sacrifice, viewed anticipatively by God. . . .; now it is clearly revealed that salvation and righteousness are received by faith in the crucified and resurrected Savior" (C. I. Scofield, *New Scofield Reference Bible* [New York: Oxford, 1967], p. 1,124; as quoted in Ryrie, *Dispensationalism*, p. 107). Likewise, Chafer wrote, "No system of merit, such as was the law, could possibly be applied to a people who by riches of divine grace have attained to a perfect standing, even every spiritual blessing in Christ Jesus" (Lewis Sperry Chafer, *Systematic Theology*, vol. 4 [Dallas: Dallas Seminary Press, 1948], p. 19). When charged with "teaching 'various plans of salvation for various groups in various ages' by the General Assembly of the Presbyterian Church in the W.S." (Ryrie, *Dispensationalism*, p. 108), Chafer replied, "The references cited by the Committee from the Editor's writings have no bearing on salvation whatever, but concern the rule of life which God has given to govern His people in the world" (Chafer, "Dispensational Distinctions Denounced," *Bibliotheca Sacra* 102 [January 1945]: 1. As quoted in Ryrie, *Dispensationalism*, p. 108).

29 Ryrie, *Dispensationalism*, pp. 121-40.

30   H.A. Ironside. See MacArthur, *Jesus*, 176. It should be noted that Gerstner accuses Ironside of antinomianism (Gerstner's pejorative term for free grace) as well and points out statements made where Ironside wrote that a true Christian can persist in the practice of sin until death, which may come early due to such sinful behavior. See Gerstner, *Wrongly Dividing*, pp. 216-17. Additionally, his passage quoted by MacArthur does not actually support Lordship salvation. Ironside was not a proponent of Lordship salvation.

31 For example: Clarence Larken, *Dispensational Truth* (Philadelphia: Larkin, 1918) and *Rightly Dividing the Word* (Philadelphia: Larkin, 1918), Charles Ryrie, *Dispensationalism Today* (Chicago: Moody Press, 1965), E. Schuyler English, et al., *The New Scofield Reference Bible* (New York: Oxford University Press, 1967), L. S. Chafer, *Grace* (Grand Rapids: Zondervan, 1922) and *He That Is Spiritual*, rev. ed. (Grand Rapids: Zondervan, 1967).

32 This intention is especially clear in his statement, "Frankly, some mongrel species of dispensationalism [which he has defined as the dispensationalism of Ryrie, Chafer and others] ought to die, and I will be happy to join the cortege" (MacArthur, *Apostles*, p. 221).

33 Ibid., p. 34.

34 Ibid., p. 35.

35 Ibid., p. 219.

36 John Piper and Justin Taylor, *Stand: A Call for the Endurance of the Saints*, (Wheaton: Crossway Books, 2008), p. 129.

37 Dr. MacArthur appears regularly at the Ligonier Conferences (for a compilation of his lessons, see: "John MacArthur Resources," available online at: <http://www.ligonier.org/learn/teachers/john-macarthur/>; Internet; accessed 11 June 2017), and has appeared at the Desiring God National Conference twice. (For a compilation of his messages, see: "John MacArthur," available online at: <http://www.desiringgod.org/authors/john-macarthur>; Internet; accessed 11 June 2017). These conferences both primarily feature proponents of covenant theology.

38 MacArthur, *Apostles*, p. 221.

39 Rightly understood, *antinomianism* is the doctrine that righteous living is not important. Free grace, on the other hand, teaches the importance of righteous living, while keeping it distinct from justification before God.

40 John Gerstner, *A Primer on Dispensationalism* (Phillipsburg: Presbyterian and Reformed Publishing Co., 1982), pp. 2-6.

41 Gerstner, *Wrongly Dividing*, pp. 86-87.

42 Gerstner, *Primer*, p. 5.

43 See especially, John Gerstner, *Wrongly Dividing*, pp. 105-147.

44 Ryrie correctly asserts, "If plain or normal interpretation is the only valid hermeneutical principle and if it is consistently applied, it will cause one to be a dispensationalist. As basic as one believes normal interpretation to be, and as consistently as he uses it in interpreting Scripture, to that extent he will of necessity become a dispensationalist." Ryrie, *Dispensationalism*, p. 24.

45 See Richard Mayhue, "Who is Wrong? A Review of John Gerstner's *Wrongly Dividing the Word of Truth*," *The Master's Seminary Journal* vol. 3, no. 1 (Spring, 1992):73-94. While I do not accept Mayhue's argument that dispensationalism and TULIP Calvinism are not incompatible, the article does well to point out the methodological flaws in Gerstner's book.

46 See also Kimbro, *The Gospel According to Dispensationalism*. Kimbro's thesis is that dispensationalism is a system of soteriology first. This work is especially relevant because Kimbro writes from a historic premillennial viewpoint, demonstrating that it is more than dispensational eschatology that has an impact on soteriology.

47 Including, *The Redeemer's Return* (Santa Ana, CA: Calvary Baptist Church Bookstore Publishing, 1970); *The Golden Age: A Treatise on the One Thousand Year Reign of Christ on Earth* (North Kingstown, RI: Historic Baptist Publishing, 1994); *The*

Antichrist (Eastford, CT: Martino Fine Books, 2011); and *The Prophetic Parables of Matthew 13* (Covington, KY: Kentucky Bible Depot, 1946).

48 Pink, *The Redeemer's Return.*

49 Ibid., p. 219. Emphasis in original.

50 Ibid., p. 43.

51 Ibid., p. 43.

52 Ibid., p. 42.

53 Ibid., p. 210, emphasis in original.

54 Ibid., pp. 209-12.

55 Ibid., p. 178, emphasis in original.

56 Arthur Pink, *Studies on Saving Faith,* (Swengel: Reiner Publications, 1974), p. 12.

57 Ibid., pp. 156-63.

58 Ibid., p. 109.

59 Ibid., p. 134, emphasis in original.

60 Arthur Pink, *The Saint's Perseverance* (Lafayette: Sovereign Grace Publishers, 2001), p. 24.

61 "It is very difficult to say which is the cart and which is the horse in this case. Is it the literalistic tendency that produces this divided Scripture, or is it the belief in a divided Scripture that drives the Dispensationalist to ultra-literalism at some point? I think it is the latter, though that is not easy to prove" John Gerstner, *A Primer on Dispensationalism* (Phillipsburg: Presbyterian and Reformed Publishing Co., 1982), p. 5.

62 Many on both sides think that this minor 'hermeneutical' difference [between literal interpretation of prophecy and non-literal interpretation of prophecy] is a more foundational difference than the theological. We profoundly disagree for we believe that the Dispensational literal hermeneutic is driven by an a priori commitment to Dispensational theological distinctives." John H. Gerstner, *Wrongly Dividing the Word of Truth: A Critique of Dispensationalism* (Brentwood, TN: Wolgemuth and Hyatt, Publishers, Inc., 1991), pp. 86-87.

63 Literal interpretation does not mean that figures of speech are not recognized, but that the original intention of the author, and that alone, is sought. Conversely, to stop seeking the original intention of the author is to cease from literal interpretation, even if an allegorical method is not used.

64 Stanley Toussaint and Charles Dyer, editors (Chicago: Moody Press, 1986), pp. 35-48.

65 For points 1-4 see Ryrie, *Dispensationalism* (Chicago: Moody, 2007), pp. 45-48. For point 5, see *The Ryrie Study Bible: New Testament New American Standard Version*, (Chicago: Moody, 1977), pp. 273-74 (notes on Rom. 7). See also Alva J. McClain, *Law and Grace: A Study of New Testament Concepts as They Relate to the Christian Life* (Chicago: Moody, 1991).

66 Even among dispensationalists that interpret the sermon as a description of ethics during the kingdom dispensation, this is not properly considered a prophetical sermon, but a manifesto.

67 Compare Joseph Dillow, *The Reign of the Servant Kings: A Study of Eternal Security and the Final Significance of Man* (Haysville, NC: Schoettle Publishing Company, 1992), pp. 433-66; and Arthur Pink, *An Exposition of Hebrews* (Grand Rapids: Baker, 1968).

68 See John F. MacArthur, *The Gospel According to the Apostles* (Nashville: Word Publishing, 1993, 2000), pp. 105-138.

69 See John F. MacArthur, *The Gospel According to Jesus* (Grand Rapids: Zondervan, 1988, 1994), pp. 31-33, 96-97.

70 David R. Anderson, *Free Grace Soteriology* (NP: Xulon Press, 2010), p. viii.

71 For example, the sheep and the goats judgment in Matthew 25:31-46 is distinct from the great white throne judgment. The sheep and goats are separated before any works are mentioned and then judged separately according to works. The non-dispensationalist sees this as a description of the one judgment where all men will appear to determine eternal destiny. With this basis, the view that works are necessary to escape everlasting punishment cannot be avoided. For contrasting views regarding this judgment, see (the dispensational view) Stanley D. Toussaint, *Behold the King: A Study of Matthew* (Grand Rapids: Kregel, 1980), pp. 288-92; and (the non-dispensational view) David Hill, *The New Century Bible Commentary: The Gospel of Matthew* (Grand Rapids: Eerdmans, 1972, 1981), pp. 330-32.

72 See Edmund K. Neufeld, "The Gospel in the Gospels: Answering the Question 'What Must I do to be Saved?' from the Synoptics," *Journal of the Evangelical Theological Society* (June 2008), p. 272. "The first eight beatitudes (Matt. 5:3-10) attract our reader, because each gives a condition and a reward, and the reward generally sounds like eternal life." Matthew 5:5, for example, presents the reward for the meek, "*autoi klēronomēsousin tēn gēn*," meaning literally, "they will inherit the land." The dispensationalist understands that this has to do with possessing the land promised to Abraham in the Abrahamic Covenant (Gen. 15:17-21) in the kingdom. If there is no literal land to possess, as the amillennialists believe, it is understandable that they believe that this "generally sounds like eternal life." The dispensational premillennialist does not confuse the two and has no problem here.

73 This latter view also makes works a condition for spending eternity with God.

74 See, for example, John Gill's exposition of Zeph. 3:13 in *Exposition of the Entire Bible* available online at: <http://www.biblestudytools.com/commentaries/gills-exposition-of-the-bible/zephaniah-3-13.html>; Internet; accessed 10 October 2011.

75 "The No True Scotsman fallacy involves discounting evidence that would refute a proposition, concluding that it hasn't been falsified when in fact it has.

If Angus, a Glaswegian, who puts sugar on his porridge, is proposed as a counter-example to the claim 'No Scotsman puts sugar on his porridge', the 'No true Scotsman' fallacy would run as follows:

> (1) Angus puts sugar on his porridge.
> (2) No (true) Scotsman puts sugar on his porridge.
> Therefore:
> (3) Angus is not a (true) Scotsman.
> Therefore:
> (4) Angus is not a counter-example to the claim that no Scotsman puts sugar on his porridge."

Author unknown, "'No True Scotsman' Fallacy," available online at: <http://www.logicalfallacies.info/presumption/no-true-scotsman/>; Internet; accessed 30 June 2016. Note that the "Real-World Examples" given in the conclusion of this article are specifically relevant to this discussion.

76 Supralapsarianism is the view that election to salvation and reprobation to destruction precede the fall in the logical order of the Divine decrees. In other words, according to supralapsarianism, sin was introduced as a means to accomplish election and reprobation.

77 See R.T. Kendall, *Calvin and English Calvinism to 1649* (Oxford: Oxford University Press, 1979, 1997), pp. 51-66.

78 This chart is available online at: <http://www.reformed.org/calvinism/index.html?mainframe=/calvinism/perkins.html>; Internet; accessed 1 July 2011.

79 *The Justification of God: An Exegetical and Theological Study of Romans 9:1-23,* (Grand Rapids: Baker Books, 1993), pp. 64-65.

80 Neufeld, p. 271.

81 Ibid., p. 270.

82 "Matthew 8:1-25:30 . . . has not altered the offer of life to those who hear the golden rule and obey it, to those who leave all to follow Jesus. Active obedience to Jesus and his teaching continues to be the narrow gate to life" (p. 277, emphasis added). "Our reader also finds God working graciously in these chapters [Matt. 8:1-25:30], but generally not in a way that overturns the emphasis on active obedience being rewarded with salvation" (p. 277, f.n. 26, emphasis added). "Following Jesus requires surpassing loyalty than that to family and to life itself, and Jesus' words make these conditions essential

for receiving eternal life" (p. 288), and "The Third Gospel usually speaks of receiving eternal life in terms of some active obedience. This includes being merciful, being more loyal to Jesus than any other in the face of opposition, even to losing one's life, and living obediently to Jesus" (p. 290, emphasis added).

83 Neufeld, p. 268 (emphasis in original).

84 I would like to point out that I do not believe Neufeld wants to intentionally misrepresent the theology of the synoptic writers. In fact, his article reads like an honest attempt to understand the synoptics by a writer that is uncomfortable with trying to maintain the contradictory views of justification by faith alone and justification by works and has essentially chosen the latter. It must be instead that he fails to recognize that intended audience and authorial intent are inseparably related. This seems to me to be the primary exegetical pitfall of proponents of Lordship salvation. Because they see the purpose of history as soteriological, all passages must fit into that box, no matter the context.

85 I would like to point out that this also seems to be the root of the confusion about what dispensationalists have taught regarding the justification of Old Testament saints. While the dispensationalist is discussing their salvation in reference to theocratic privilege, physical and material blessing, possession of the land, etc., the covenant theologian naturally assumes salvation from the penalty of sins is in view. Dispensationalists have never taught that in the Old Testament justification before God in an eternal sense was by anything other than faith alone, but dispensationalists have made many statements that sound that way to covenant theologians who are applying the hermeneutics of covenant theology to their words. We are simply speaking different languages. See, for example, Gerstner's discussion of this problem in *Wrongly Dividing*, pp. 149-69.

86 MacArthur, The Gospel According to Jesus, p. 96.

87 It should be noted that ironically even in Luke 19:10, Jesus is not discussing an evangelistic intent. It should be understood that this passage refers instead to bringing wayward believers back into obedience to the Shepherd.

88 John Piper, *Desiring God: Meditations of a Christian Hedonist* (Sisters: Multnomah Publishers, Inc., 1996), pp. 65-66. Piper is a premillennialist and has a strong focus on the glory of God in his writings, nevertheless, he is consistent in interpreting the Bible through a lens of individual salvation from the penalty of sins.

89 While the LXX does not use the words *anapsuxis*, "refreshing," or *apokatastasis*, "restoration," a related word (*apokathistēmi*) does appear in Acts 1:6 regarding the kingdom and the concept is clearly present referring to the kingdom in Isaiah 48:6-8, Ezekiel 37 and many other passages in the prophets. As McClain states: "Reflecting now upon the total content of Acts 3, it is hard to imagine how words could have made any plainer the historical reality of this reoffer of the King and His Kingdom to the nation of Israel" (Alva J. McClain, *The Greatness of the Kingdom: An Inductive Study of the Kingdom of God* [Winona Lake: BMH Books, 1974], p. 405). See also the whole context of his discussion of Acts 3 on pp. 403-406.

90 MacArthur also makes this significant oversight. *Apostles*, pp. 33, 196.

91 A good example is the discussion on justification in Romans 1 to 4 setting up the discussions on sanctification in chapters 5-8, dispensationalism in chapters 9-11 and liberation in chapters 12-16.

92 For example, Luther endeavored to maintain a clear distinction between law and grace. Martin Luther's work *Christian Liberty* (Philadelphia: Luther Publication Society, 1903) is considered a classic work in drawing this distinction. In it he wrote: "A Christian man needs no work, no law, for his salvation; for by faith he is free from all law, and in perfect freedom does gratuitously all that he does," p. 33.

93 Daniel P. Fuller, *Gospel and Law: Contrast or Continuum?* (Grand Rapids: Eerdmans, 1980), p. 6. I would only want to amend this by stating that while the law was exclusively for Israel, grace is not exclusively for the church, but for all people of every age who believe.

94 It should be noted that progressive dispensationalism maintains this theme of continuity as well and also places the Christian under the law. For example, Turner states, "Matthew portrays the church as a Jewish community whose mission is to summon all the nations to obey Jesus, the ultimate Torah teacher who fulfills Moses and the prophets. Matthew's Jewish church is distinct from Israel only because of its messianic faith, and the church today is redemptively continuous with these Jewish roots." David L. Turner, "Matthew Among the Dispensationalists," *Journal of the Evangelical Theological Society* Vol. 53, No. 4 (Dec 2010):714. And "[Recognizing the Church's Jewish roots] equips the church to fulfill its role as the vehicle through which Torah, as fulfilled through the instruction and example of Jesus, is extended to all the nations of the earth" (p. 715).

95 Arthur Pink, *The Law and the Saint* (Grand Rapids: Christian Classics Ethereal Library) available online at: <http://www.ccel.org/ccel/pink/law.pdf>; Internet; accessed 12 October 2011. Emphasis in original. While I would agree that the Old and New Testaments are not antagonistic, this does not lead to Pink's conclusion that the law is applicable to the Christian.

96 MacArthur, *Apostles*, pp. 59, 120.

97 Ibid., p. 119. As McClain adeptly observes, "To emasculate the law of God of its divine penalties and still call it 'law' is a serious misnomer. It can only confuse the minds of men and finally bring all law, whether human or divine, into contempt or indifference. Moreover, eventually such a procedure tends to empty the cross of Christ of its deepest meaning. The law loses its absolute holiness, sin loses its awful demerit and Calvary loses its moral glory." *Law and Grace*, pp. 11-12.

98 MacArthur, *Apostles*, p. 117.

99 Ibid., p. 134. It is odd that someone who claims that, "Those who think they are Christians but are enslaved to sin are sadly deceived" (Ibid., p. 120) can at the same

time say that Romans 7:23 ("But I see another law in my members, warring against the law of my mind, and bringing me into captivity to the law of sin which is in my members") describes "every true believer." This seems like a description of slavery to sin to me. Ironically, Lordship salvation and binding the Christian to the law inevitably lead to this kind of acceptance of sin.

100 While this chapter did not separately address the impact of denying the distinction between the church and Israel, maintaining this distinction is necessary for maintaining the points of dispensationalism that were addressed here.

101 Many dispensational distinctives were held by the early church fathers, and some aspects can be found in Protestant writers as far back as the early 17th century. However, this chapter will be limited to the discussion of dispensationalism after it was formerly systematized by J.N. Darby (around 1828).

102 "Who are the defenders of no-lordship dispensationalism? Nearly all of them stand in a tradition that has its roots in the teaching of Lewis Sperry Chafer. I will show in Appendix 2 that Dr. Chafer is the father of modern no-lordship teaching. Every prominent figure on the no-lordship side descends from Dr. Chafer's spiritual lineage. Though Dr. Chafer did not invent or originate any of the key elements of no-lordship teaching, he codified the system of dispensationalism on which all contemporary no-lordship doctrine is founded. That system is the common link between those who attempt to defend no-lordship doctrine on theological grounds." John F. MacArthur, Jr., *The Gospel According to the Apostles*, (Nashville: Word Publishing, 2000), p. 35.

103 Lewis Sperry Chafer, *He That Is Spiritual* (Grand Rapids: Zondervan, 1918, 1967, 1983).

104 Lewis Sperry Chafer, *Grace: An Exposition of God's Marvelous Gift* (Grand Rapids: Zondervan, 1922, 1972).

105 Lewis Sperry Chafer, *Systematic Theology* (Dallas, TX: Dallas Seminary Press, 1948).

106 Regarding this latter point, it has been noted by many that John Calvin also taught assurance apart from works. However, due to the combination of his doctrine of perseverance with double predestination and federal theology, this concept fell away in Calvinistic circles shortly after Calvin. That one could have assurance based upon the promises of Christ alone without examination of his or her works was largely (there were a few exceptions) absent from theological discourse in the 17th through 19th centuries. By contrast, dispensationalist teachers vigorously argued that assurance based upon the promises of Christ alone was essential to the Christian life. For the early roots of the view that assurance comes through careful consideration of one's works, see R.T. Kendall, *Calvin and English Calvinism to 1649* (Oxford: Oxford University Press, 1979) and M. Charles Bell, *Calvin and Scottish Theology: The Doctrine of Assurance* (Edinburgh: The Handsel Press, 1985).

107 Later in the same article, Mackintosh seems to repudiate limited atonement. In

addition, in an essay entitled, "God For Us," he wrote, "When we have from the lips of our blessed Lord Himself, the eternal Son of God, such words as these, 'God so loved *the world*,' we have no ground whatever for questioning their application to each and all who come under the comprehensive word 'world.' Before any one can prove that the free love of God does not apply to him, he must first prove that he does not form a part of the world, but that he belongs to some other sphere of being. If indeed our Lord had said, 'God so loved a certain portion of the world,' call it what you please, then verily it would be absolutely necessary to prove that we belong to that particular portion or class, ere we could attempt to apply His words to ourselves. If He had said that God so loved the predestinated, the elect, or the called, then we must seek to know our place amongst the number of such, before we can take home to ourselves the precious assurance of the love of God, as proved by the gift of His Son. But our Lord used no such qualifying clause." *The Mackintosh Treasury: Miscellaneous Writings by C.H. Mackintosh* (Sunbury, PA: Believers Bookshelf Inc., 1999), p. 607. Emphasis his. Clearly, Mackintosh rejected limited atonement.

108 Ibid., p. 605.

109 Ibid.

110 This last point was the cornerstone of Robert Govett's (1813-1901) ministry and continued with those whom he influenced, including D. M. Panton, Watchman Nee and G. H. Lang. Likewise, Chafer did devote some pages to discussion of the bema in *Systematic Theology*, vol. III, pp. 307-309; vol. IV, pp. 396 and 404-6; and vol. VII, p. 296. However, the judgment seat of Christ to determine reward was somewhat absent from the Plymouth Brethren and Presbyterian dispensationalists, and did not become heavily influential in mainstream American free grace theology until Zane Hodges. See below.

111 J. N. Darby, "No More Conscience of Sins," available online at <http://www.stempublishing.com/authors/darby/EVANGEL/12018E.html>; Internet; accessed 1 March 2012. See also Darby, "The True Grace of God in Which You Stand," *Journal of the Grace Evangelical Society* (Autumn, 1995):69-73.

112 Mackintosh, "The Christian: His Position and His Work," *The Mackintosh Treasury*, p. 670, emphasis his.

113 "Perhaps the father of American dispensationalism was James Brookes. . . . Brookes wrote the book *Maranatha*, which achieved wide distribution as it popularized a dispensational view of prophecy. . . . Perhaps Brookes will best be remembered as the one who introduced C.I. Scofield to Dispensationalism shortly after his conversion." Thomas Ice, "A Short History of Dispensationalism, Part III," *Dispensational Distinctives* (May-June 1991), p. 1. Scofield said of Brookes, "During the last twenty years of his life Dr. Brookes was perhaps my most intimate friend, and *to him I am indebted more than to all other men in the world for the establishment of my faith*." Ernest Sandeen, *The Origins of Fundamentalism*, Historical Series no. 10 (Philadelphia: Fortress Press 1968), p. 223. As quoted by Larry Crutchfield in *The Origins*

of Dispensationalism: The Darby Factor (Lanham, MD: University Press of America, Inc.), p. 17. Italics supplied by Crutchfield.

114 James Hall Brookes, *Salvation: The Way Made Plain* (Philadelphia: American Sunday-School Union, 1871), 123-484. Available online at: <http://books.google.com/books?id=aRgHAAAAQAAJ&pg=PP1#v=onepage&q&f=false>; Internet; accessed 1 March 2012.

115 Ibid., p. 445.

116 Ibid., p. 283.

117 See Robert Govett, "Tracts on the Kingdom No. 4: The Gift and the Prize" in *Kingdom Studies* (Miami Springs, FL: Schoettle Publishing Co., 1989), pp. 1-6.

118 Space does not permit a proper treatment of the significance of the *Scofield Reference Bible* (Oxford: Oxford University Press, 1909), but it should be noted that it was instrumental in the grassroots rise of dispensationalism and was for many the first exposure to the sharp distinction between law and grace (see note on John 1:17), the idea that James 2:14-26 was discussing justification before men (see note on Jas. 2:24), and the idea that the sermon on the mount was a manifesto for the Messianic kingdom intended in primary application to the Jews (see note on Matt. 5:2).

119 D. M. Panton, *The Judgment Seat of Christ* (Hayesville, NC: Schoettle Publishing Co., 1984), see especially pp. 3-4.

120 William Kelly, "The 'Well of water springing up into everlasting life,'" available online at: <http://www.stempublishing.com/authors/kelly/6h_s/hs2_well.html>; Internet; accessed June 11th, 2017.

121 J. N. Darby, "Reflections Upon The Prophetic Inquiry and The Views Advanced in It," *The Collected Writings of J. N. Darby, Prophetic* No. 1, Vol 2. Available online at <http://www.plymouthbrethren.org/article/11495>; Internet; accessed 1 March 2012.

122 J. C. Ryle, *Holiness: Its Nature, Hindrances, Difficulties, and Roots* (Grand Rapids: Baker, 1979, 1981), p. 59. Emphasis in original. This work was first published in 1883 by William and Hunt Co.

123 Charles Hodge, *Systematic Theology*, vol. III, *Soteriology*, (Peabody, MA: Hendrickson, 2008), p. 238. This work was originally published in 1845.

124 Robert L. Dabney, *Discussions of Robert Lewis Dabney*, Vol. 1 (Carlisle, PA: The Banner of Truth Trust, 1891, 1967, 1982), p. 179-80. Emphasis in original.

125 Lewis Sperry Chafer. 1948. "The Spiritual Life, Lesson 1," Lectures on the Spiritual Life. MP3 file. <http://raystedman.org/mp3/4321.mp3>; Internet; accessed 5 January 2012]. Italics mark verbal emphasis.

126 Bell, Scottish Calvinism, p. 9.

127 Calvinists avoid the charge of salvation through human merit by seeing the initial repentant faith as a gift, and perseverance in faith and works as guaranteed by God to all the elect. But this does not lessen the fact that in this system these are conditions which need to be met in order to fulfill one's end of the covenant and if anyone does not meet these conditions they will be damned.

128 To this could be added the peace covenant (Ezek. 34:25-30), but this covenant it not mentioned often in Scripture and is almost entirely absent from the dispensational literature on covenants. For this reason, the discussion will be limited to the other covenants.

129 Also related to the Abrahamic covenant is what is sometimes called the *land covenant*, described in Deuteronomy 29:1-30:20. While Israel will indeed be restored to the land promised in the Abrahamic covenant (Ezek. 37:1-25; Jer. 33:19-26), I do not see this passage as expressing a separate covenant. Instead, it is a part of the blessings and curses of the Mosaic covenant described in Deuteronomy 27 to 30, which states that Israel will be restored to the land after dispersion if they return to the Lord. See especially Deuteronomy 30:1-3.

130 By contrast, lordship salvation proponents echo the language of the early federalists when they speak of saving faith as something we exchange or trade with God for everlasting life. It is not difficult to see that the argument which says free grace makes it too easy is nonsensical if faith is not something which is traded for everlasting life.

131 To avoid confusion, I must point out that the law was never able to give Christ's life (Gal. 3:21), and that justification never could be through the Law (Rom. 3:19-20). This was simply not the law's purpose.

132 J. N. Darby, "Deliverance from Under the Law, as Stated in the Holy Scriptures." Available online at <http://www.stempublishing.com/authors/darby/DOCTRINE/07007G.html>; Internet; accessed 5 February 2012.

133 Alva J. McClain, Law and Grace: A Study of New Testament Concepts as They Relate to the Christian Life (Winona Lake, IN: BMH Books, 1954, 1967), pp. 44-45.

134 L. S. Chafer, *Grace: The Glorious Theme* (Grand Rapids: Zondervan, 1922, 1950), p. 233. Regarding the law of Christ, see chapter 1 in this present work.

135 This unbiblical term is becoming more common in theological discourse and seems to be the logical result of Lordship salvation.

136 Zane Hodges, (Chicago: Moody Press, 1972).

137 This curriculum is available in print and is used by many churches. Grant Hawley, *The Guts of Grace: Preparing Ordinary Saints for Extraordinary Ministry* (Allen, TX: Bold Grace Ministries, 2013).

Dispensational Publishing House is striving to become the go-to source for Bible-based materials from the dispensational perspective.

Our goal is to provide high-quality doctrinal and worldview resources that make dispensational theology accessible to people at all levels of understanding.

Visit our blog regularly to read informative articles from both known and new writers.

And please let us know how we can better serve you.

Dispensational Publishing House, Inc.
PO Box 3181
Taos, NM 87571

Call us toll free 844-321-4202

Lightning Source UK Ltd.
Milton Keynes UK
UKHW020856011220
374377UK00010B/2147